I LOVE YOU
RITUALS

I LOVE YOU RITUALS

Becky A. Bailey, Ph.D.

HARPER

NEW YORK · LONDON · TORONTO · SYDNEY

HarperCollins books may be purchased for educational, business, or sales promotional use. For information, please write: Special Markets Department, HarperCollins Publishers Inc., 10 East 53rd Street, New York, NY 10022

FIRST EDITION

Designed by Nancy Singer Olaguera

Printed on acid-free paper

Library of Congress Cataloging-in-Publication Data
Bailey, Rebecca Anne.
   I love you rituals / Becky A. Bailey
      p. cm.
   Includes bibliographical references and index.
   ISBN 0-688-16117-0
      1. Parent and child. I. Title.
HQ775.85.B333 2000
306.874—dc21   00-040883

09 ❖/RRD 30 29 28 27 26 25 24

This book is dedicated to this very moment; may we all choose to experience it.

Contents

Acknowledgments   xi

Chapter 1   **Boosting Your Child's Brain Potential:**   **1**
           The Four Vital Goals of I Love You Rituals

Chapter 2   **I Love You Rituals and Disciplining**   **23**
           Children: A Powerful Connection

Chapter 3   **Getting Started and Ensuring Success**   **37**

Chapter 4   **Positive Nursery Rhymes**   **57**

           A Wonderful Woman Who Lived in a Shoe   59

           Peter, Peter, Pumpkin Eater   62

           Twinkle, Twinkle, Little Star   63

           Little Miss Muffet   65

           Humpty Dumpty   67

           Georgie Porgie   69

           Margie Pargie   71

           Mary Had a Little Lamb   72

           Little Bo Peep   74

Hot Cross Buns   76

Mary, Mary, Extraordinary   79

To Market, to Market   81

Wee Willie [Wendy] Winkie   83

Jack Be Noodle   85

Ba Ba, Black Sheep   87

Three Nice Mice   89

Chapter 5   **Interactive Finger Plays**   **91**

Dancing Hands   93

Five Little Babies   96

Growing Up   99

Here's the Beehive   101

Here's the Bunny   103

Mr. Sun   105

On Your Face   107

One, Two, Three, Four, Five   109

Round and Round the Garden   111

There Was a Little Mouse   112

Ten Little Candles   114

The Hello Game   117

This Little Finger   119

This Little Finger Goes Night-Night   122

Today Is _____'s Birthday   123

Two Blackbirds   125

Warm Hands   128

You Have Ten Little Fingers   130

Your Fingers Are So Sleepy   133

You've Been Gone   136

Contents

viii

Chapter 6 **Silly Interactions**   **139**

    Family Handshakes   141

    My Hand Is Stuck   143

    Greetings   144

    What Did You Bring Home from   145
    School Today?

    My Face Has a Gift for You   146

    Silly Me   148

    Jelly Bean Toes   149

    Yes and No Game   150

    You Have a Present   151

    Mama's Smart Girl [Boy]   152

Chapter 7 **Soothing and Relaxing Games**   **153**

    Goodnight Elbow   155

    Guess What I Am Writing [Drawing]?   156

    Hot Dog Game   158

    Putting Lotion on the Hurts   160

    Tell Me When I Am at the End   162

    Rub and Dry Game   163

    Move What I Touch   165

    Story Hand   167

Chapter 8 **Hide-and-Seek Games**   **169**

    Find the Stickers   171

    Find the Yarn   173

    Hello, Toes/Good-bye, Toes   175

    Can You Find It?   176

    I'm Hiding   178

    Peek-a-Boo. I See You!   180

    Where Are Those Hands?   181

    Where Did It Go?   183

Contents

ix

Chapter 9 Cuddling and Snuggling Games   **185**

Snuggle Time   187

Blanket Swing   188

Row, Row, Row Your Boat   190

Snuggle Up   192

Held in My Arms   194

Chapter 10 Physically Active Games   **195**

Blanket Volleyball   197

Cotton Ball Blow   199

The Big Crash   201

The Cat and the Bunny   202

Walk and Stop   204

Bibliography   205

Index   206

Contents

Acknowledgments

In my own journey in working with disadvantaged children and those children who have experienced a number of life's challenges, Dr. Pat Clark, friend and colleague, and I began studying Developmental Play by Dr. Viola Brody and Theraplay®* by the late Ann Jernberg. I am indebted to the wisdom of these great women. Studying their work was a life-changing experience for me. Each of these approaches requires adults to be present, in the moment, engaged with children. If you had asked me earlier in my life, "Becky, do you believe you are truly present with children when you interact with them?" I would have responded with a definite yes. I came to discover that this was not accurate. I, like many of you, have been socialized to think either of the past (what I should have done) or the future (what I need to do next). The present was an elusive commodity for me.

As I began my personal journey, I found out something very surprising: I was frightened of the present moment. This understanding was inspired by the work, friendship, and love of Carol Howe. The saying goes, "When the student is ready, the teacher appears." This was the case with Carol, who is my

---

*The Theraplay Institute, 1137 Central Ave., Wilmette, IL 60091

teacher, mentor, and friend. The present was where my feelings were located. I had spent so many years staying busy, exercising, achieving, and taking care of others; I never realized these were different forms of compulsion to drown out my feelings. I also thought that if I relaxed and let down my defenses, people would see me as incompetent or unworthy. What I discovered, with Carol's guidance, was that when I chose to relax and be in the present, I felt connected and loved. My fears melted away. The more I could stay in the moment, the more I could engage with children. Just think about it. If young children live in the present and adults spend most of their time in the past or in the future, we have abandoned our children to some degree.

This book, *I Love You Rituals,* came out of my journey from being lost in the past and projecting my thoughts into the future to rediscovering myself in the present. I once read, "The true gifts of life lie in the moment. That is why we call it the present." We, as a culture, have replaced presence with presents.

Each moment we have a choice to be fully present and loving or available yet disconnected. I Love You Rituals were created in my moments with children. They have truly been gifts to me. I have had the privilege of connecting with some wonderful children, all of whom demanded, in their own way, that I stay present with them. For those children and the moments we spent together, I am thankful. The vast majority of these songs and chants I learned during my childhood or were taught to me over the years by children, parents, or teachers. Every effort has been made to locate the creators and authors of these rhymes and give them due credit. I am grateful to the generations of people who have kept these fingerplays and activities, some of which go back hundreds of years, alive.

As with any endeavor, this book came about through a synergy of people and events. I originally sat at the computer to work on a book entitled "Conscious Discipline." Instead, this book is what came forth. I was blessed with inspiration and am appreciative. I want to acknowledge my godchild, Etta June, who played many of these rituals with me and helped me more clearly define the hand positions. Kate O'Neil willingly stood in as a guinea pig if no child was available. She taught me the value of these experiences for adults as well as children. Jeff Jones shared his artistic talents by drawing the illustrations. Toni Sciarra, my editor, has been as much a mentor as an editor. She is a master listener. Her ability to reflect back to me what I thought I was saying brought clarity. With this clarity came peace. I am deeply grateful for her skills and talents. Thanks to Gareth Esersky, my literary agent for believing in the work.

Dr. Robert Schuller once called me "my new friend Becky Bailey." I am grateful to Dr. Schuller who indeed has been a true friend in supporting my work. His positive message has inspired and helped me as well as millions of other people.

Finally, I would like to thank those people in my life who taught me about rituals—my family and friends. I am deeply grateful to a group of friends affectionately called the "Longwood Ladies." They were the first to teach me about ritual. Thank you, Mom and Dad, for your consistent gifts of love. To my second mother, Ellen, you are a treasure, and Dot, thank you for your faith and love. To Lucas, thank you for allowing me to be a part of your life.

When I was younger, I used to get pains in my stomach. My Grandmother Canipe would have me lie on the couch, and she would sit down in such a way that I would curl around her. As the pains eventually disappeared, I continued to sit with her on the couch in this fashion. I watched television while she snapped beans. It became an "I love you ritual" for us. To this day when I curl on the couch to watch television, I reconnect with her. I am so grateful for those moments, and even though she passed away over twenty-five years ago, through our ritual her presence is still with me. These I Love You Rituals are my present to your presence. Good journey!

Chapter
1

Boosting Your Child's Brain Potential: The Four Vital Goals of I Love You Rituals

From a little spark may
burst a mighty flame.

—Dante

I Love You Rituals are delightful interactions and games that adults can play with children from infancy through eight years of age and that send the message of unconditional acceptance. Unconditional acceptance is love.

Imagine arriving home to be greeted by your spouse. His or her eyes light up as you enter the house. You begin to talk about your day, and you receive your spouse's complete attention. Simultaneously, your spouse begins to give you a deep hand massage that sends invisible cellular messages coursing like radio waves throughout your body. The messages are, "You are safe, you are adored, all is well." In this loving state, you become attuned to the wonders of life and the passion of living, and the world becomes a positive place where each person has untold value. What a wonderful interaction that would be. What a powerful display of love. This greeting sure beats the heck out of, "What's for dinner?" or "Did you pick up the dry cleaning?" I Love You Rituals are gifts of love you can give your children. Since what you give to others, you strengthen in yourself, they are gifts you can give yourself.

Take a deep breath and read the following aloud:

> A wonderful woman lived in a shoe.
> She had so many children
> She knew exactly what to do.
> She held them,
> She rocked them,
> And tucked them in bed.
> "I love you, I love you,"
> Is what she said.

Reflect on your emotions. How do you feel after reading the rhyme? Now take another deep breath and read the original Mother Goose rhyme:

> There was an old lady who lived in a shoe
> She had so many children she didn't know what
>   to do.
> She fed them some broth without any bread

And whipped them all soundly and sent them to
   bed.

Reflect on your feelings once again. What word would you use to describe how you feel after reading this rhyme? This simple exercise vividly demonstrates that what you see, hear, and sense affects your brain, and your brain governs your physiology, your feelings, and your behavior. It is time to create new rituals, rituals that reflect our worth and extend love to others.

It is one thing to revise the old Mother Goose rhymes, but I Love You Rituals are much more than that. They are rituals that send the message of unconditional love to children. Unconditional love is something we all seek to find and hope to give. This unconditional love is sent in what I call "child language" through I Love You Rituals. It is sent in a game, in words, and through touch, and it is sent repeatedly. The playfulness of the game is crucial, for in play, children and adults are totally present, absorbed in the moment. Think about watching your children play. They become so engrossed in their actions, you can't get them to notice you or the call to supper. Pay attention to yourself when you play. For some of us, reading is play. We become deeply drawn into the story, easily staying up to 2:00 A.M., losing track of time. Those of us who enjoy tennis or other forms of play lose ourselves in the activity. In this flow of activity, we find a precious part of ourselves and feel rejuvenated.

THE GOOD NEWS ABOUT THE TRAGEDY AND VIOLENCE WE SEE

Over my twenty-five years of working with children and families, I have noticed a growing undercurrent of change. Viewed from a small perspective, this change could appear disruptive or negative; yet from a bigger picture, its beauty is unfolding. From a microscopic view we see increases in juvenile delinquency, suicide, rebellion, depression, apathy, and drug addictions. In young children, we see enormous increases in hyperactivity, impulsiveness, power struggles, demanding behavior, and willful fits of displeasure when they do not get what they want. In young adults, brilliance and genius are budding, yet a moral compass is missing. Busy, frantic parents chase dreams and miss moments with each other and with their children. Others work to make ends meet and spend little time with each other. Material goods seduce us more than kindness. News headlines offer tragedy after tragedy, so that denial becomes a defense against hopelessness. But under all these struggles, all these cries for help, is a rumble, a wave building in the ocean of life, ready to crest and carry us all forward. This rumble is our intense, true desire for connection with each other. We long to belong. We strive to offer and receive unconditional love. This desire to be loved and loveable unites us all.

We are shifting from being families and communities based on roles to groups based on healthy relationships. The role of wife had certain duties, the role of husband had required obligations. The role of the child to be seen and not heard was paramount. These roles of days gone by offered security. Yet that security was riddled with oppression, lack of freedom, and rigid rituals that served the powerful, not the many. The roles provided security without connection. These roles had to crumble; they needed to fall. In this process, turmoil, crisis, pain, confusion, and hopelessness reign as families scramble to hold together and marriages fail more often than not. However, our souls seek to overcome these strivings and are ready to connect with each other in a different capacity, on an equal footing. To move from roles to relationships, we have traveled from self-hatred, shame, and guilt to acceptance of ourselves and each other. We progressed from the rigidity of sameness to tolerance of differences, from fearing change to embracing its potential. We are shifting from living in the past or the future to living in the present. We are returning to love. On the outside, it looks like the end of the world is coming, but on the inside, we are pulling together as never before. This book is about getting together. It is about reconnecting with ourselves and our children. In these cute activities and rituals you will be conducting with your children, you will find something very precious—yourself. These I Love You Rituals are needed now in our culture. They are our bridge from roles to relationships.

Win-Win Activities

One guiding truth about life is that what you offer to others, you strengthen within yourself. Stop reading this book for a moment. Think about your children and how much you love them. If they are at school or a room nearby, just wish them well. From your mind and heart, allow the feelings to overflow and send them a silent blast of love. Now, how do you feel yourself? Probably warm and cozy. You offered your children love and security by wishing them well, and you yourself welled up with love. The same is true when we offer criticism and blame. When we see what is lacking in others, what they are not doing, and what is wrong with the world, we simultaneously feel lacking. You cannot go through your day seeing what is wrong and go to bed happy. Self-esteem does not come from how others see you, but from how you see others. Thus we can see the power of the Golden Rule. It is golden because it affects both parties. See the beauty in others, and you can see the beauty in yourself. By conducting these I Love You Rituals with children, not only do you boost your child's brain potential, but you heal your old wounds. Parents, aunts, uncles, grandparents, stepdads and stepmoms all find love for themselves as they extend love to their children. I Love You Rituals ground you in the present moment, connect you with your children, and help you reestablish and maintain a safe place within from which love radiates.

I Love You Rituals

ROUTINES VERSUS RITUALS: THE NEED FOR BOTH

Life with young children is full of routines. There are bedtime routines, chores routines, and mealtime routines, to mention a few. Routines are essential for young children. Routines help children learn to tell time and regulate their own internal clocks. Children discover that after bath time comes story time. They learn to predict what will happen next, and in doing so, they feel more empowered to tackle the task. Our brains are pattern-seeking devices. The clearer the patterns for young children, the more brain-enriching the environment. This explains why many parents of young children return from vacations exhausted. When the routine for the child changes, chaos and grumpiness can fill the space previously occupied by routines.

Rituals are not routines. There is a difference between the two. The goal of routines is continuity. The goal of rituals is connection. Rituals create sacred space designated for togetherness and unity. Holiday rituals typify this point. Many families gather on Thanksgiving to bond in gratitude, and birthday rituals, such as having one's favorite meal prepared, are a form of honoring a family member. Rituals are the glue that holds the mosaic of love together. Street gangs create rituals to fill the emptiness their members feel as a result of the lack of connection in their lives. We can create healthy rituals with our children, or they will form them with others as best they can. Just as in the earlier example of greeting your spouse, we can greet our children with an I Love You Ritual, or we can arrive at the day care center and say, "Where are your things? Hurry; we have to stop at the store on the way home." The choice is ours.

Loving, healthy rituals foster the development of loving, emotionally healthy children. This book is about creating and building healthy rituals.

THE FOUR GOALS OF I LOVE YOU RITUALS

Delightful and cute as these activities are, they are designed to accomplish four vital goals.

Goal 1: I Love You Rituals optimize your child's brain for success at school and in life.

These activities are designed to increase your child's attention span and cooperation. The amount of time you spend locked in power struggles and hearing such phrases as, "I can't," "I don't have to," "You can't make me," and "I don't care" will decrease. I Love You Rituals can literally change your child's brain chemistry.

Life boils down to the ability to communicate. Brain cells communicate with each other via chemical molecules called neurotransmitters. Neurotransmitters act, to some degree, like on-off switches creating communication pathways between cells, similar to wires linking telephone poles. If these neurotransmitters do not function optimally, communication within the brain is disrupted. This disruption is reflected in your child's behavior.

Dopamine,* a key neurotransmitter, supports our brain in a number of ways. First, symbolically dopamine says, "Focus on this; pay attention." It helps us stay focused. How often do you feel that your child is inattentive? How "spacey" do you feel at times? Coffee increases the efficiency of dopamine, which is why some people feel sharper after that first cup. Second, dopamine motivates us to achieve our goals. It says, "Go for it; get what you desire." Dopamine helps us take action toward achieving our goals, rather than passively wish things were different. Dopamine also is instrumental in creating the positive emotions we feel when we experience successful social interactions. After a delightful lunch with friends, for example, we feel satisfied and content. This, to some degree, is the afterglow caused by dopamine. Years ago, a movie called *Awakenings* showed the devastating effects of life without dopamine as the character portrayed by Robert De Niro sat frozen in a wheelchair, unable to move, focus, or interact with others.

The dopamine system appears to be "jump-started" and calibrated in the early years of life. Such games as peek-a-boo, patty cake, and blowing raspberries are linked to the development of the dopamine system. The secret ingredients appear to be eye contact, touch, and the bonding these interactions provide. Watch a caring adult interact with a six-month-old infant: Their eyes meet, and a connection is made between them. It is similar to later experiences we call love at first sight. Adults and infants take turns imitating each other's facial expressions, one leading and the other following as in a graceful ballroom

---

*Dopamine performs many functions within the body. A full discussion of its contributions is beyond the scope and purpose of this book.

dance. The allure of this mutual intimacy overrides the self-consciousness of even grumpy adults. "Gitsy-goooo," creeps out of the mouths of even the most reserved adult in the presence of an adorable, responsive baby.

I Love You Rituals are designed to foster eye contact and bonding. In the process, the dopamine system of children is strengthened, as are attention span and social development. All are integral to your child's social, emotional, and school success.

Children who are surrounded by chronic bickering or tension at home may learn to tune out the unpleasantness to survive. This process of tuning out can be a reflection of lowered dopamine levels in the brain. A few years ago a friend brought her family to Disney World for a vacation. After a day in the heat and crowds, they returned to their hotel room to meet me for dinner. When I arrived, my friend and her husband were in the middle of an argument. Their ten-year-old son was stoically staring out the window, his facial expression unfocused. He was doing what all of us have done at one time or another: He was "becoming invisible" and removing the fight from his perceptual field. He was relieving the tension by lowering his ability to attend and thus depressing his dopamine level. Chronically low dopamine levels, if not corrected, can create problems throughout life. Such problems may include

1. a short attention span
2. the inability to concentrate and follow through on tasks
3. hyperactivity
4. a lesser ability to read the social cues of others

I Love You Rituals provide daily tune-ups for your children, through which attention spans are likely to increase and cooperation improve.

Try the following experiment. Notice what your child does when your relationship with him or her is disrupted by a series of conflicts. You will notice that your child's eye contact with you becomes minimal and that when you reach out to touch your child, your overture is rebuked. The child pulls away from you, resisting reconnection. When relationships are in need of repair, eye contact is one of the first social actions to go, followed by touch. The journey to reconnection comes through communication. Communication occurs through the simultaneous engagement of eyes, touch, and loving words—all of which are provided in I Love You Rituals.

Goal 2: I Love You Rituals increase your learning potential and effectiveness through touch.

Touch is the only sense we cannot live without. Your child could be blind and be fine, she could be deaf and be okay, but without touching and being touched, a child will die. In 1920, Dr. Henry Chapin, a New York pediatrician, reported that the death rate for infants under two years of age in institutions across the United States was 100 percent. These infants received adequate food and shelter. What was missing for these babies was caring touch. Chapin concluded that being handled, carried, cuddled, and caressed was necessary for life. Experiments continue to support Dr. Chapin's conclusions. Research indicates that in animals and humans alike, the behavior of those who receive caring touch is strikingly different from that of those who don't. All animals (including humans) who received large quantities of caring touch were relaxed, cooperative, had strong immune systems, possessed an overall better functioning physiology, were friendly, and were better able to handle all forms of stress. The animals who did not receive adequate touch were timid, apprehensive, and high-strung. They were frequently tense, hyperresistant, impulsive, anxious, irritable, and aggressive. With millions of our children on Ritalin, youth violence rising, and social skills declining, one cannot help but wonder about the relationship between the time allotted for caring touch and current educational and parenting practices.

When I conduct workshops with parents, touch is an integral aspect of the experience. Often I sense the participants' discomfort. "I could do this easily with my children. I just find it difficult with another adult," they frequently say. These comments are usually made by women. Many men simply refuse to engage in the activities at all. We have created many rationalizations to explain why we are not to touch one another. The fears are numerous. In recent decades, the United States underwent an important period in which we became aware of the damage wrought by sexual abuse. This was a necessary step in our evolution. Sadly, however, we then added the specter of sexual abuse to the list of "why" we don't touch. We have become a society of untouchables. It is becoming much easier to shop and buy presents for one another than to give or receive a hug. Young infants are placed in infant seats to be carried, in car seats to be transported, and in bassinets to sleep. We are becoming trained to touch babies only when they demand our attention. With time the commodity most sought by modern parents, a quiet baby who is willing to entertain herself in the infant carrier frees parents to attend to life's other demands. Unfortunately, as we focus on other demands, our children are becoming demanding.

Touch is much more a metaphor in our society than a reality. When we speak of someone who is removed from reality, we say that he is "out of touch." We speak of people who have a "magic touch" or a "professional touch." We speak of someone who is quick to take offense or overly sensitive as "touchy." We never really feel secure unless we can "hold onto something," nor do we really believe that we understand anything until we have a "firm grip on it." I Love You Rituals give us permission to move from the symbolic expression of touch to caring touch. Somewhere, somehow, we have lost "touch" with ourselves and our children. We have grown so distant from each other that permission to touch one another and a structure for doing so are necessary steps in our return to health.

Brain research confirms the critical role of touch in our mental and emotional health. When we touch one another, a hormone is released called the nerve growth factor. This hormone is essential to neural function and learning. The brain and the skin develop from the same embryonic tissue. The skin, in essence, is the outside layer of the brain. If we want smart, happy children, we must consciously touch them. It is time to relearn appropriate, caring touch and move past our fear of inappropriate touch. We must embrace touch for its value and function in development and learning.

By understanding caring touch, children develop compassion for themselves and others. Hitting becomes hugging, snatching becomes asking, and the difference between caring touch and unwanted, uncomfortable touch is learned. Touch is the keystone of each of the I Love You Rituals in this book.

Years ago I was visiting my grandmother in a nursing home. When I arrived, she seemed unaware of who I was. She said, "Does Mamma know where I am? I haven't been home today." I assured her that her mother knew exactly where she was and that all was well. Most of the time during our visit, she spoke as if she were a young child. Every now and then, she would become aware of the present and notice that someone was wearing a pretty red dress or a red sweater. I felt deeply sad and found it hard to start a conversation with her. So, I decided to conduct some I Love You Rituals. I told my grandmother, "I am going to do some things with you that you did with me when I was little." I took her hand. I did as many I Love You Rituals that involved the hands as I could think of. After about fifteen minutes of "playing and touching," her eyes became alert, she looked right at me, and said, "Becky, how is everything at the university?" That was my last connection with my grandmother, and I am grateful I had that moment. I urge you not to let this book sit on a shelf.

Goal 3: I Love You Rituals create loving rituals that hold families together even through the roughest times.

All cultures across time have created rituals. Rituals are a central part of life, whether they involve how meals are shared or how major events and holidays are marked. Rituals surround us, from the common birthday ritual of making a wish before you blow out the candles to bedtime routines that may include, "Sleep tight, don't let the bedbugs bite." Rituals create time to be playful, to explore the meaning of our lives, and to rework and rebuild relationships. Think of the pleasant rituals from your childhood. What feelings are evoked as you allow yourself to reminisce? Generally, they are feelings of love, warmth, and safety. For these moments, "all is well" with yourself, your family, and the world. One woman I know shared her ritual of "sniffing" her granddaughter when they hugged each other. She would wrap her arms around her granddaughter, put her nose on her granddaughter's neck, and inhale as if to breathe in the child's essence. As silly as this ritual may sound, the meaning it holds for both grandmother and granddaughter will last a lifetime.

It is striking how different families are today from twenty-five or fifty years ago. As our society restructures itself with shifting gender roles, blended families, cultural diversity, and economic and political uncertainty, fear is a prevalent emotion. New rituals are needed for families and for children. I Love You Rituals put life in focus, shifting our attention from getting ahead to getting together; from valuing material wealth to valuing one another. They are called "rituals" because they are designed to be part of the day-to-day activities between adults and children.

Rituals are moments taken solely for the purpose of connecting. Rough transitions during the day or week signal times when a ritual is needed. A child who is being picked up from school may whine, complain, or bicker with you or siblings in the car. A calming ritual or a change in rituals is needed. Picking up children at school with the words, "Hi, how did it go? Where's your coat? Do you have your homework? Hop in the car, we need to stop at the store. Come on. Hurry up. I don't have all day," doesn't reconnect you with your child. Instead, try the "What Did You Bring Home from School Today?" ritual on page 145. This ritual would involve meeting your child and saying, "There you are. I've been waiting all day to hug you. Let me see what you brought from school. You brought those brown eyes. You brought that cute little mole on your arm. You brought your backpack and coat. Let's go."

Reflect on the times during your day when you think, "I need someone to focus just on me—someone to love me, notice me, and adore me." Those times are screaming for an I Love You Ritual. I Love You Rituals are perfect for reconnecting with children when you pick them up from school, after you return from a business trip, on waking your children in the morning, or when tucking them in bed at night. Pick a time, pick a place, and consistently engage your child in these activities every day. The loving ritual has then begun.

Though I Love You Rituals are essential for all children, they are critical for children who have experienced loss in their lives. These losses include moving; leaving homes, neighborhoods, and schools; divorce; death of family members (including pets); and birth of siblings. These rituals ground children when change threatens them.

Goal 4: I Love You Rituals strengthen the bond between adults and children that insulates children from drugs, violence, and peer pressure, laying the foundation for mental and emotional health.

The bond between parent and child is the child's primary source of emotional health. It gives your child the capacity to have satisfying relationships the rest of his or her life. A weak or anxious bond could reverberate through your child's entire life in the form of low self-esteem, impaired relationships, and the inability to seek help or ask for it in effective ways. Research indicates that over one-third of the children in middle-class families suffer from anxious attachments to their parents. This insecure attachment tends to be transmitted from one generation to another. Every parent wants to know what early experiences enable a child to feel that the world is a positive place. We ask ourselves how a child becomes equipped with enough confidence to explore, to develop healthy peer relationships, and to rebound from adversity. We seek to know what builds a child who sees himself or herself as being loved, loving, and valuable. We wonder, "Do I have what it takes to raise a secure child? What can I do to support my child or change myself?" Today, with parents spending less time in the home and families being reconstituted in new shapes and combinations, it is time for some I Love You Rituals. We need this anchor; the seas are choppy.

Secure attachment is created by the subtle quality of adult-child interactions. It does not happen because a parent holds, feeds, bathes, or responds to an infant's cries. It is based on *how* the adult responds. We have all had the experience of talking with a spouse or friend who looks as though he or she is listening, but something is missing. We have gone to the movies and out to dinner with a friend, having a reasonably good time, but sensing that something is missing. Conversely, we have had experiences with spouses and friends when we felt that a wholeness was present—that they were truly "there" and that we were attuned to the moment and each other. This connection is at the heart of our bonding with children and with each other.

The following stories demonstrate the difference between responding to the physical needs of a child and bonding with the child by responding to his or her emotional needs.

Once, as I was eating lunch with a dear friend at a restaurant, we noticed a twelve-month-old boy at the table behind us. He was excitedly banging his spoon on his tray and delighting in the movements of his arm and the sounds he produced. Sarah, my friend, said to the boy, "There you are, We see you," and she imitated his arm going up and down. His face lit up and his eyes locked on Sarah's as the connection between them formed.

Then two firetrucks passed the restaurant, sounding their alarms. The loud noise and flashing lights distressed the child. His brow furrowed, his lips began to quiver, and he appeared to be on the verge of tears. However, he made no attempts to check his mother's expression for information or reassurance, as would be typical for young children. Young children up to age four or five rely on the parent's affect, or demeanor, to determine whether a situation is safe. Later in life, they can discern this information themselves by environmental clues. This child's mother was busy putting on the child's jacket, collecting the diaper bag, and gathering stray objects thrown from the highchair. That is, she was busy with the physical demands of the situation. The child needed reassurance and information from his mom that all was well. This information, delivered through eye contact, was not given, leaving the child to his own minimal resources. The emotional needs of the child were not noticed. This mother was attending to the mechanics of mothering but was not attuned to her son.

While at the neighborhood park, a young boy was sliding down the slide head first. At the end of his ride, he shot off the ramp like Evil Knievil and landed on his elbows and chin. Both elbows were scraped, and his chin was cut and bleeding. The boy began to wail. He made no effort to look for his mother or search her out. This behavior is not typical of children his age, so I watched closely. His mother promptly retrieved him and carried him to the picnic table where she was sitting. The boy continued to cry. He sat stiffly on the picnic table as his mother rummaged through her handbag looking for a tissue. As she pulled out the necessary items to treat the wounds, she began lecturing him in a nonstop, mechanical way about listening to her, going down the slide feet first, and other rules she thought could have prevented this accident. The mother had attended to the cuts, not to the child's emotional needs. I understood why the child had not sought out his mother upon being injured.

At a toddler center, a young child was determined to play behind the changing table—an area that was off-limits to children. The caregiver said in a loud, somewhat threatening voice, "Oh, no, you don't. Get out from behind here. Now GO!" The toddler burst into tears. The caregiver's response was, "I am not impressed with those tears." She was attending to the rules of the child care center, not to the emotional needs of the child. By saying, "Come here, Adam. It is not safe behind the table. We can play together over here," she could have attended to both the rules and the child.

In our hurried society, many are finding the mechanics of parenting all they can handle. The joy of parenting is lost. Parents are overwhelmed with the pressures of modern life. These demands create times when parents are sometimes physically absent and other times when our bodies are present but our minds are elsewhere. The ramifications of our well-intentioned absences may manifest themselves in certain behavioral characteristics in our children. We may see our children acting like bullies, taking advantage of more vulnerable children. Or we may see them victimized and excluded by others or excluding themselves to manage their anxiety about failing. We may see our children being impulsive or shy, showing poor concentration skills, getting easily upset, and lacking initiative. Or we may see rampant independence that hardens into stubbornness and bossiness. We may see our children struggle with friendships, jealous and afraid that they may lose the security of a best friend. We might see them shy away from risk and group activities or leap in and take unsafe risks. We might believe these behaviors are part of the child's genetic temperament. Temperament is a factor; however, brain research indicates that although nature provides the raw materials for brain development, nurture is the architect. How we interact with our children profoundly shapes their brains. We literally custom design our children's brains. Many of the behaviors we see can be traced to the original bonding experience between children and their caregivers.

As daunting as it may seem, there is hope. Just as children are forgiving, so, too, is the brain—especially in the early years. The brain can be shaped and reshaped by each new experience; like a house that gets dirty, a good cleaning is all it needs. I Love You Rituals are designed to strengthen the bond between an adult and a child and, in turn, reestablish the child's sense of security. This secure base then frees the child to explore the world with greater willingness and success. It also builds healthy ties between the adult and child, increasing the child's willingness to be cooperative. Imagine that you are sitting on your couch at home with your spouse. Lately your relationship has been going very well—communication and connection are at an all-time high. If one of you were to get up and the other asked, "Honey, while you are up, would you get me a sandwich?" more than likely the answer would be, "Sure, what would you like?" Now pretend you are on the couch and the relationship is going poorly—so poorly that you wonder why this person is sitting on *your* couch. Suppose one person gets up and the other asks for something. The likely response would be, "Get it yourself; you have legs."

Cooperation is directly related to the connection we feel with each other. The same is true with children: Strengthen the bond and increase the cooperative spirit.

The four goals of *I Love You Rituals* are attainable for you and your child. You will optimize your child's brain development, increase his or her learning potential, strengthen your family, and lay the foundation for your child's emotional well-being.

HELP FOR CHALLENGING CHILDREN

Not all children pop out of the womb easily able to settle and sleep, cuddle, and enjoy sustained interactions. Children have different temperaments. Those of you who have more than one child are aware of the differences between them. Some children handle change well, and some children were born anxious. Some children are persistent and focused, and some are "all over the place." Your child may be struggling with attention deficits or hyperactivity. As I noted earlier, changes in family structure and location can create challenges for children. Some challenges that could profoundly affect your child include these:

1. Divorce or unresolved marital tension
2. Death of a parent or family member
3. Parents with addictions
4. Adoption
5. Birth of siblings
6. Changing homes and schools
7. Medical issues (chronic ear infections, colic, and the like)

For children with challenges, I Love You Rituals are like life preservers for sailors adrift in dangerous seas. They help children move through storms. Unless children are helped to deal with challenges, they may challenge adults by demonstrating a myriad of irritating behaviors. To children with challenges, life seems frighteningly out of control. Some children become resistant in an attempt to put the brakes on life events. "You can't make me" and "I don't have to" are common phrases. Other children attempt to control by being controlling. This bossiness is challenging for you, teachers, peers, and siblings. Children who are happy see other children as possible friends. Children who are hurting see other children as competition for scarce resources. Regardless of the form the resistance takes, these children do not trust the world enough to feel optimistic and open.

I Love You Rituals are modeled after the social games parents play with infants—games in which two people interact to produce possible continued interaction. Think back to when your child was an infant. Whether you were changing diapers or preparing a feeding, a game of peek-a-boo could emerge out of nowhere. The game lasted as long as it lasted and then vanished just as quickly as it began. You really never knew how long the game would last, but what mattered was how much you both enjoyed the game at the moment it was happening. That enjoyment was the certainty; the thing you both could count on. A level of uncertainty exists in all social interactions. We never really know what will happen: Will the interaction produce a positive response? Will the interaction be sustained or cut short? To thrive in the world, we must learn to tolerate a level of uncertainty. Some children react to uncertainty with anxiety. Adults sometimes feel the same way; they prefer some guarantee of outcomes before they risk interactions. By playing I Love You Rituals with your children, you replace mistrust of the outcome with trust. Anxiety about the uncertainties of life abates and is tempered by a growing ability to live in the mystery, anticipating delight rather than fright.

In addition to the four general goals *I Love You Rituals* help to accomplish, the rituals have the following significant benefits:

1. They keep the child at an optimal level of arousal. Have you noticed that some children have trouble modulating their arousal system? They are easily upset, and once they are frustrated, they have a difficult time regaining their composure. I Love You Rituals are designed to build relationships that help children internalize or adjust their arousal system to a more even level.

2. They provide the child with a feeling of control over the environment, which fosters self-confidence and promotes intellectual growth. Have you noticed that some children are always seeking to gain control over other people, situations, or events? I Love You Rituals encourage interaction

based on the dance of responsiveness: As the adult is responsive to the child, the child learns to become responsive to others. In this dance, the child learns a feeling of control that comes from within, not from controlling outside events.

3. They expose the child to intense social interactions that promote attachment and provide the basis for all other social and communication skills. Have you noticed that some children do not have the skills needed to get along with other children? They have trouble making and sustaining friends, taking turns, and sharing. I Love You Rituals are interactive games that become the platform from which turn taking and sharing evolve.

4. They encourage the child to engage his or her surroundings. Have you noticed that some children have stereotypical forms of play? They tend either to play the same games repeatedly or to move impulsively from toy to toy without truly getting involved in play. I Love You Rituals allow the child to experience successful engagement with a caring adult. The adult directs the game, extending the child's abilities to attend and focus.

5. They attune the child to the social aspects of language. Have you noticed that some challenging children have speech delays? I Love You Rituals are generally face-oriented games. The games increase the child's ability to focus on the face of the adult. With this focus, the child becomes more attuned to the part of the body that produces speech, assisted by the "hints" provided by facial expressions.

How often do you get caught up in the daily agenda, making lists of what to do, losing sight of your own and others' deepest needs? We attend to the dishes, laundry, carpool, phone calls, and faxes, but not to each other. Attending to the subtle nuances of our children is at the heart of what is called the attachment process. Through the attachment process, the parent-child bond is formed. This bond is the foundation of all emotional health. Release the guilt of what could have been or should have been and get started NOW with *I Love You Rituals*.

Take a deep breath and commit yourself to do these rituals with your child on a regular basis. Watch your child blossom in your presence and heal from unintentional absences. The healing of ourselves, of each other, of our children, and of society begins one bond at a time.

Chapter
2

I Love You Rituals
and Disciplining Children:
A Powerful Connection

The main source of good discipline is
growing up in a loving family, being loved
and learning to love in return.

—Benjamin Spock

Imagine having a fight with your significant other. You argue over how to discipline your child, *again*. From your perspective, your partner's techniques seem a bit harsh. From his perspective, you are a wimp, babying the child into incompetence. These arguments continue day in and day out as the child grows. Earlier in the marriage, you did things together, and communication was good. The arguments about child rearing were manageable because the relationship was going well. Forgiveness was given freely. Ten years later, it seems as if the only communication left is the arguments. In a rocky relationship, the conflicts seem larger than life. They siphon hope from the relationship the way leeches suck blood. Bitterness and resentment take the place of forgiveness. Complaining, silence, or being right becomes more important than connecting. As sad as this story is, it paints the picture of the connection between discipline and being in relationship with others. The stronger the relationship, the more willing each party is to be cooperative.

Discipline comes from the word "disciple," which is rooted in the Latin word that means to teach. Opportunities for discipline occur during moments of conflict between the needs and wants of the parties involved. You may want and need your child to be in bed by eight o'clock, but your four year old wants to watch late-night television. These needs collide to create moments of discipline for parents. How we resolve these moments "teaches" our children how to resolve conflicts for the rest of their lives. It models for them how to treat others who disagree with them, how to handle being disagreed with, and how problems are to be solved. The stronger the connection between parent and child, the greater the chances that conflict will be respectfully resolved.

I have always thought that discipline is similar to the country-western dance called the two-step. The dance consists of two steps: the slow-slow and the quick-quick. In the case of discipline, the quick-quick step of discipline involves asking the question, "What do I do or say right this minute to solve this problem?" The slow-slow step involves asking the question, "How do I keep my relationships as healthy as possible so that the desire to be cooperative is maximized?" *I Love You Rituals* are the slow-slow step of disciplining children.

UNCONDITIONAL LOVE: RELATIONSHIP VERSUS REWARDS

Each of us wants to give unconditional love to children, yet we frequently find ourselves setting limits and conditions on children's behavior and activities. We are constantly giving commands and reminders: "Get in your car seat, put on your seat belt, finish your homework, pick up those toys." We find ourselves repeatedly saying no: "You may not play in the street, you can't have any candy, stop hitting your brother." We seem to spend a lot of time saying or implying, "If you do _____, then you may _____." Sometimes the fun activities children enjoy are used as rewards; therefore, they, too, become conditional: "If you finish your homework, then you may play with your friends."

If we take an honest look at a day with our children, we can see that the amount of unconditional attention we give them is minimal. Think about all the things you do with and for your children. From this mental list, remove all the things that you feel you have to do (as part of your responsibilities as a parent or grandparent), all the things you do out of guilt because you think you fell short of your obligations, and all the time you spend reminding or disciplining your children. How much time is left for the sheer enjoyment of each other? How many interactions are truly unconditional? If you are like me, those moments occur when the child is sleeping. We gaze at our sleeping little ones, overflowing with love for them. What we feel when they wake up and dawdle getting dressed, however, is a different matter.

Discipline and guiding the behavior of young children are difficult tasks for most adults. I Love You Rituals are an integral part of any disciplinary approach you may choose. Take a moment and think about this next sentence very carefully: *The motivation to behave comes from being in relationship with one another.* Historically, we believed that to motivate children to behave in ways we approve of, we had to make them feel bad. We removed privileges, sent them to time out, shouted, and lectured. Modern approaches attempt to motivate children to behave through rewards: "If you get in the car right now, I'll take you to McDonald's." Children are offered material goods, from smiley-face stickers to money, as rewards for acceptable behavior. Research indicates that the side effects of such systems are deadly to a democratic society. When adults govern children's behavior through outside motivators, they teach children "other control." A democratic society needs people who have self-control—who have the intrinsic desire to be cooperative. Rewards teach children to value material goods and to approach a task asking, "What's in it for me?" They teach children to focus on the result and ignore the process. Getting an A on a report card, not learning, is the goal.

I hear many adults say, "What harm could be done by giving rewards? That is the way the world works. I get paid for the job I do." My response is this: "Who would you rather have build your house? The person who is there only to get the paycheck, or the person who loves building and, as a result, earns money for her talents?" I have had the former build a house for me, and I am still finding problems that need to be fixed. Rewards reduce intrinsic motivation in children. In essence, they erase the work ethic.

Eric Jensen (1997), leader in the field of brain-compatible practices, states that the brain operates differently when it is motivated by rewards than when it is intrinsically aroused. The anxiety triggered by the threat of not getting the rewards we dangle in front of children releases chemicals in the brain that can inhibit creativity, problem solving, and recall. New research also indicates that the use of rewards may hinder children from learning how to delay gratification.

Most adults want children to be cooperative members of a family. We want children to "choose" to behave well and to be internally motivated to care about others. If we bribe our children with goods to be good, however, we are not teaching them the value of caring; we are teaching them to look out for themselves. If you have ever watched the nightly news and asked yourself, "How could a corporation be more concerned about profit than the safety of our drinking water?" or "How could a business ignore the needs of its workers to turn a profit?" you will not want to be a parent who relies on rewards to control your children. Your dissatisfaction will eat at you until you scream, "There must be a better way!" We can make time to give unconditionally to our children and develop healthy relationships. These healthy relationships become the foundation of the child's internal drive to be caring and productive. Or we can rely on rewards. The choice is ours.

TWO COMMON MISTAKES ADULTS MAKE

Many of us find ourselves making two common disciplinary mistakes, as follows:

1. We get caught up in our obligations and tasks and lose sight of our children until they "get in trouble" (displease us) or "do something special" (please us). On these occasions, children receive our undivided attention—negative or positive. Neither type of attention is helpful or healthy. Children come to learn that to be "loved" (that is, to get attention), they must either misbehave or be special. These two positions require them to be less good than others (in trouble) or better than others (winning). Vacillating between feeling less than others or better than others becomes a vicious cycle. Ironically, one of the reasons adults get caught up in excessive obligations is their need to avoid feeling less good than others or to feel better than others to maintain their sense of self-esteem. To break this cycle, adults must take charge and establish strong relationships with children. They must make time to "be" with their children. This time must be commanded and orchestrated by adults, not demanded by children. I Love You Rituals can be the beginning of the process by which adults regain control of themselves and stay in charge of children.

2. Often, we find ourselves locked in negative patterns of interaction with our children. As the children grow and challenge the adults around them, constant battles can become the norm, rather than the exception. These battles can be especially trying during the toddler years. Toddlers may say no or be resistant to a parent nine times an hour. This resistance can make for long days. As these battles continue, day in and day out, the relationships between the

adults and children become strained. After the battles are over, both the adults and the children often feel guilty about their actions. Or they feel guilty for not acting. Either way, guilt becomes the prevalent emotion.

Permissive parenting always follows guilt. Permissive parenting is an epidemic in our society. It is the tendency to give in to your children's demands, make exceptions to previously established rules, or not follow through on consequences, all with the goal of avoiding conflict. However, giving in to your children creates more problems because it trains the children to be obnoxious to get what they want. By giving in, we no longer mean what we say and say what we mean. Our communication becomes dishonest. After a while, when we look into our children's eyes and say, "I love you," our children can no longer trust that we mean that, either. Without this trust, our children's behavior becomes more and more demanding.

Thus, the question is, How do we "make up" with our children without "giving in" to them? What will heal the relationship after mistakes are made? The answer is I Love You Rituals. When your relationship with a child has become challenging, make time for an I Love You Ritual in the morning and in the evening. As you add these moments of unconditional love to your relationship, you will be inviting cooperation back into your home. You will transform your guilt into active healing of the relationship instead of giving in to your child in an attempt to seek his or her forgiveness for your actions that you perceived were neglectful or inappropriate.

RECLAIM YOUR PARENTAL POWER

We often hear it said that children need to learn to respect authority. This statement is true. Authority comes from the word "author." To find out who has authority in a given situation, ask yourself, "Who is the "author" of this experience for me?" If you believe that your children are driving you nuts, you are saying that they have the power to create your feelings for you. They become the author of your life. You have given away your authority to them.

Recently I was in the car with a friend, driving to see some property he was interested in purchasing. At every traffic light, my friend became irritated. He would fuss and fume at the red lights, grump and complain over the yellow lights, and be sarcastic with the green lights ("Well it's about time!"). He was choosing to let himself be driven nuts by the traffic lights. I thought to myself, "This is what traffic lights do." Why did he want to be a nut? Why do any of us want to be a nut? Why do we give our power away to traffic lights, children, or spouses? What is so attractive about choosing to be a victim?

Whenever you believe that someone or something other than your perception has made you angry, happy, sad, or guilty, you give your power away. Whomever you have put in charge of your feelings you have put in charge of you. You give up your authority. When you give up authority, you give up respect along with responsibility. The upside is that you get to blame others for your upset. The downside is that you feel powerlesss. You start believing that if others can make you do things that you don't want to do, then you should be able to make others behave in certain ways, too. Both these beliefs are myths.

The belief that adults can make children behave or get them to change is common. This pressure creates enormous guilt in parents, since making others change is ultimately impossible. Remember, guilt fosters permissive parenting. Certainly, we can threaten someone into submission; however, you have probably met children who do not respond to threats, removal, loss of privileges, or other forms of control. No matter how much pressure we put on children to behave, it is ultimately their choice to submit their will to us. Their choice to be cooperative is embedded in our relationship with them, not in our manipulative strategies.

The message that one person can make others think, feel, and behave in certain ways is taught daily. Comments such as, "Look what you made me do! Now I am late for work," or "Look how you made your brother feel. Was that nice?" are common. "Don't make me have to call your father" or "Don't make me have to take away that video game" are equally common phrases heard in families. When we put one person in charge of another, we teach other-control, not self-control. Other-control—the desire to control others, rather than yourself—then runs rampant in our marriages and relationships with children. It destroys communication and, like a tornado, leaves devastation in its wake. It is time for a change.

To change, we must first change our beliefs and then change our practices. Take a deep breath and affirm to yourself, "The only person I can *make* change is me." Then instead of saying, "Look what you made me do! Now I am late for work," you may say, "I feel frustrated and embarrassed going to work late. I need your help in the morning to get out the door on time. Will you help me?" Instead of saying, "Look how you made your brother feel. Was that nice?" you could say, "See your brother's face? He looks sad" and teach your child how to read the nonverbal cues of others. These statements reclaim your power by making you the author of your experiences.

When you withdraw your energy from *making* children behave, you will free yourself to focus on building the relationship you want with your children. You will be the "author" of your life. This is how you teach your children to respect authority. This is how you model self-control.

Noticing: Wiring Your Child's Brain for Self-Control

The brain needs feedback. Every parent knows this. Listen to children negotiate for feedback from adults: "Look, Mom, I can stand on one foot. Look! Look!" As soon as you notice them, you hear, "Watch me do it again!" I live in Florida. I would love to have a dime every time I heard a child say, "Watch me jump into the swimming pool!" The child's need to be seen is usually far greater than the adult's patience. Sometimes the child's plea for "just one more time," sounds like a broken record.

The brain loves feedback because it *needs* it to survive. In her book, *Enriching Heredity: The Impact of the Environment on the Brain,* Miriam Diamond presented research that underscored the importance of enriched, stimulating environments in helping brains develop. Her research revealed that the "best" brains are those that receive immediate and high-quality feedback. The quest then becomes to understand what is meant by high-quality feedback. In general, the following guidelines about feedback will steer you in the most effective direction:

1. The more often a child receives feedback, the better.
2. The more specific the feedback, the better.
3. The more immediately the feedback is given, the better.
4. The more you notice and less you judge, the better.

What all these guidelines boil down to is that you must notice your child. If a child is standing on one foot shouting, "Look at me, look at me," our job as parents would be to say, "Look at you standing on one foot!" If the child jumps into the swimming pool, we could say, "You did it. You jumped into the swimming pool, feet first, with your hands up like this." This is not what usually occurs. Some parents look up and say "Uh, huh," while many parents say, "Good job, honey," or "That was a great jump." We mistakenly believe that if we praise our children with judgments of how good, great, and wonderful they are, we will build their self-esteem. This is not the case. *Judging our children's actions*—"Aren't you the best one-foot stander alive! Go show Grandma how good you are,"—is different from *noticing:* "Look at you; you have one foot up like this, and you are holding your hands out to your side."

Imagine you are playing softball, and it is your turn at bat. The ball is pitched; you swing and hit a home run. Coach A says to you, "Great hit." Coach B says to you enthusiastically, "Wow, you kept your eye on the ball and really shifted your weight on that follow-through. You smacked it way over the fence." Which coach helped you become more aware of yourself and your success, as well as how to repeat it? Noticing helps children become aware of themselves. This awareness wires the brain for self-control. This feedback is brain food. In contrast, judging helps children become aware of *our* view of the world, not theirs.

We notice infants without any difficulty. Parents can be heard saying, "Look at this little finger." If a baby sticks her tongue out or makes a noise with her lips, what does the adult do? We imitate; we notice. As the child gets older, noticing decreases and judging increases. An outgoing four year old who says, "Watch me!" is transformed into an anxious eight year old who asks, "Is this OK? Am I doing it right?" As a university professor, I was always amazed at the anxiety displayed by my college students. They were constantly trying to figure out "what I wanted." They would ask, "How many pages do you want?" or "Could you look at my work to see if I'm on the right track?" I would respond, "Take as many pages as you need to make your point." This would push some students over the edge into believing that I had a secret agenda. They felt sure that I had an ideal, a judgment of the way things were supposed to be, and they were bent on figuring out my reality, not theirs. Spending one's life trying to live up to the judgments of others is a disappointing journey many of us have traveled. Wouldn't it be nice to give our children a different legacy? We can do so by noticing.

As you are playing the I Love You Rituals, notice your children. Watch their faces. If they look at you, say, "You're looking right at me." If they hold their hands up to play the game, notice that by saying, "You held your hands up just like this (imitate with your hands what the children did). If you finish the game on one hand and they hold out their other hand, say, "You held your other hand up." If their faces light up with delight, notice it. Say to your child, "Your eyes got big and your eyebrows went up like this (make your face match the child's face)."

Have you ever felt, "I give my child plenty of attention, and it just never seems enough. She is always asking for more."? When children receive attention in the form of noticing, they find it immensely satisfying. They are seeing a reflection of the beauty that they are. I Love You Rituals give you the opportunity truly to see your child.

Noticing is simply saying what you see. It involves no value statement about what you observe. It simply describes. This is a difficult skill for many parents to learn. Most of us were raised on judgments and strive, to this day, to live up to those imaginary standards. Practice noticing as you and your child develop a diet rich in I Love You Rituals.

THE CONNECTION BETWEEN I LOVE YOU RITUALS AND DISCIPLINE

Most of the misbehavior children exhibit is children just being children. Children must test the limits. It is their job description. Through this testing, they discover the boundaries of life. They discover what is and what is not acceptable behavior in certain situations. Just as a child cannot attain a real notion of the size, color, and characteristics of an elephant only by reading about them, so children cannot be told something is "wrong" without experiencing it directly. That is just the way it is. This constant and repeated testing can be trying even to the most patient parents.

In addition, children misbehave when they have an unmet emotional need. This is true of all people; adults do the same thing. If we believe our spouse is being inattentive, we may do some really silly maneuvers to obtain attention. Not all these endeavors may be categorized as healthy and wholesome. When children feel slighted emotionally, they become demanding, seeking attention in any form they can. When they become demanding, we then seek to *make* them behave. In doing so, we create more distance in the relationship as children become defensive and resistant to our controlling tactics. If this cycle goes unchecked, both parents and children feel more and more out of control and powerless. Feelings of powerlessness result in blaming and resentfulness. Both parties feel poorly and unfairly treated. Children generally say, "It's not fair," while parents say, "I will not put up with this disrespect." These stances lead to more conflict.

The following chart outlines the vicious cycle of emotional disconnection that can occur between parents and children:

The child has an unmet emotional need
(The child feels unloved and not seen)

The child demands attention
(Negative attention is better than none at all)

The parents seek to make the child obey
(Via fear, force, coercion, or manipulation)

The child becomes defensive
(Pouting, whining, a "fresh" attitude, or noncompliance
are common)

Stress is created in the relationship
(Deepening the unmet emotional need, and the
cycle repeats)

I Love You Rituals can break this cycle by creating spaces in family life where emotional availability is guaranteed. Within this security, resistance, power struggles, and noncompliance are drastically reduced. If you constantly hear your child saying, "I don't care" or "You can't make me," it is time to break the cycle. Move your child to the top of your to-do list and make time for I Love You Rituals.

Chapter 3

Getting Started and Ensuring Success

These are only hints and guesses, hints
followed by guesses; and the rest is prayer,
observance, discipline, thought and action.

—T. S. Eliot

It is one thing to love our children, it is another thing for children to perceive the depth of our love for them. I Love You Rituals are designed to communicate love to your children. Many of us have heard comments, such as "Yes, I love you. Now go play." The words were there, but something was missing. Love says, "I rejoice in your presence, I affirm your value, and I let my thoughts of you grow, change, and evolve." To ensure that these games are indeed loving, you must do two things:

1. Remember your purpose. The goal of the activities is to join with our children. These rituals allow us to rejoice in togetherness, experience each other's beauty, and delight in the expression of love that we all are. They are not about having your children learn their body parts or which way is up or down. Learning these things are valuable subgoals, but the ultimate goal is to connect. Relax, have fun, giggle, sing, just be yourself—begin to trust that all is well.
2. Be fully present with your children. This statement seems wonderful and is our goal, but how do we do it? To be fully present, one must choose to do several specific things.

Be in the moment. Simply stated, your mind must be clear of clutter. You cannot be thinking about what to cook for dinner, how to meet a work-related deadline, or what the next line of the rhyme is. You cannot be thinking that this rhyme may be just the trick to get your child to go to bed. This clutter in your mind takes you out of the moment. Children sense your psychological departure and generally think it has to do with their inherent worth. The message they receive is not "I am loved," but "I am not worth being with. I am a burden."

See yourself and the child as complete, good enough, and totally deserving of this precious interaction. Do whatever it takes to remove all doubt in yourself and the child for these few minutes. Love travels from the worthy to the worthy. This means that to give and receive love, you must value yourself as well as the child. If need be, pretend you are the perfect parent with the perfect child doing the perfect activity at just the right time—even when you forget the rhyme. If you forget a part of the interaction, move on or make up something new.

Be accepting. If for any reason you find yourself feeling annoyed or upset while playing, stop the game. Feeling upset is a signal to you that your child is not meeting some expectation you have of him or her. You had a mental image of how the game was supposed to be played, and now it is going a little differently from what you had planned. With I Love You Rituals, the goal is not for the child to meet your expectations. The goal is to join in play, to experience total acceptance of each other, no matter what direction the interaction takes.

So, to be fully present in the moment, you must bring your mind to where your body is by clearing your mind of the constant chatter of what needs to be done or what should have been done. You must adore yourself and the child and accept whatever happens as just right. The present moment is where you find joy. If your life is missing joy, you are missing the moment.

STEPS TO PLAYING I LOVE YOU RITUALS

Step 1: Read through the game and make sure you understand it. If the game involves a rhyme, learn it. You and your child can do this together. You might say, "This looks fun. Would you like to learn how to do this together?"

Step 2: Select a time and a place to engage in your rituals. Many children enjoy knowing when and where they will receive your undivided attention. Some opportunities for rituals could include when waking up, saying good-bye, or coming together after periods of separation; during nighttime family time; and at bedtime.

Step 3: Be responsive to the child's cues. Learn to "read" the messages underlying your child's actions. Young children can communicate only through their actions; they do not yet have the vocabulary, understanding, or consciousness to express themselves any other way. You may start to play one game, and the next thing you know, you and the child have created an entirely new game that belongs to just the two of you. These games are not written in stone; they were made up. Feel free to do the same.

Step 4: Be conscious of the difference between what I call child initiative and child control. Sometimes children offer ideas to control the relationship, and sometimes they offer ideas to contribute to the relationship. Intuitively, you will know the difference. You will feel your child's bossiness and internally you will feel discomfort. You are in charge. Do not let the child control you. Two- and three-year-old children constantly test to see if they are in charge of the relationship (and therefore the world). If a child says, "We are going to play _____ and you are supposed to do it this way," you may respond, "That is a wonderful idea. I'm going to do my part this way and you can do your part the way you want." Symbolically the child is saying, "Am I in charge of you and of the relationship?" Your response is loving and gentle and says, "No, honey, I am in charge." Responding to a child's cues is not the same as letting the child control you. It is your job as the adult to set the parameters of the game. It is the child's job to be as creative as possible within those parameters. By exploring these issues together in a playful manner, you will see a reduction in the power struggles experienced outside of play time.

Step 5: Relax and have fun.

LEARNING THE LANGUAGE OF YOUNG CHILDREN

To be responsive to children, we must learn to listen to the language of their play. This means tuning in to the underlying meaning of their actions, not just their behaviors. Much of this information was taught to me by Dr. Viola Brody through her books, workshops, and personal sharing. The following are some common "games" that young children initiate. Their initiations are communications to you. It is critical that you learn how to respond to what they are really "saying."

Hide-and-seek or peek-a-boo: If the child starts a hide-and-seek or peek-a-boo game, symbolically the child is saying, "You can't see me; do you care if I am gone? Am I important enough to find?" Hide-and-seek can be initiated when the child turns away from you, looks away, or covers her face. This game also puts the child in control of when to be found, which reduces some of the child's anxiety about life. If the child is experiencing a lot of change, you may see the child initiating these kinds of behavior in a number of ways. Many two year olds, working on a number of developmental tasks, love to initiate hide-and-seek when you are trying to hurry out of the house for an appointment. They interpret constant pleas to hurry up as "I don't have time for you. I don't love you." Hide-and-seek is their way of saying, "I need to know you still love me and care enough to come find me." Sometimes young children may run and hide when you say, "It's time for bed." At this point, you could allow yourself to become upset or to say, "Where did Cameron go? I love him so. I will miss him. I may never see him again" and then pretend to cry. When Cameron reappears, rejoice and say, "There you are. There is my precious boy. I missed you. I love you so." Simultaneously, hold him in your arms and carry him to bed and begin reading or moving on with your nighttime routine. To make sure this game is not repeated the next evening, hold Cameron when you announce bedtime.

We can make time for I Love You Rituals with our children, or our children will force the issue by creatively selecting inappropriate times to play such games as hide-and-seek. I have found it better to orchestrate time for these activities, instead of creating children who demand them. You decide when you will play and invite the child to join you. You are the boss. Then if the child starts a game of hide-and-seek at the doctor's office, you could say, "It is not our time to play. Now is the time to see the doctor. You have a choice! Would you like to walk by yourself or hold my hand?"

"Chase me": The meaning of this game is similar to that of hide-and-seek. The child is symbolically saying, "Did you notice I was gone? Do you like me enough to come after me? Do you miss me?" Chase me puts the child in control. So if your child is feeling powerless, as if he or she has no say in a situation, look out. Your child may start a game of chase me in a grocery store or parking lot. To avoid inappropriate demands from your child to play chase me, orchestrate your life so that these rituals are an integral part of your day. With toddlers, take charge by initiating this game in your house or yard. Start the game by saying, "I'm going to get you." When you catch the child, say, "I got you. You ran off, and I came after you. I missed you. I love being with you." If the child initiates the game at inappropriate times (such as in a grocery store) do two things:

1. Catch the child and say firmly, "You ran off, and I came after you. It is not safe to play chase in the store. Something could happen to you. I am your dad; my job is to keep you safe. Stay by me. Hold my hand and walk with me. I felt scared when you ran away. I thought I had lost you. My heart would break."
2. Restructure the shopping experience so the child cannot run off again. Put the child in the shopping cart and give him or her helpful tasks to do to support the family.

Remember to play chase with your child on your terms in the safety of your home or backyard. This game is important, and young children love to play it. The choice becomes: Do you want to play it on your terms or theirs?

Playing baby games: Sometimes your children suggest a game that puts them in the role of a baby. This suggestion may indicate that they trust you to care for them. They feel safe enough to let down their guard—it is nice to be held and to relax and not have to act or be a certain way to please others. A child may also symbolically be asking, "Do you love me as much as the new baby?" Such children are longing to return to a time with no worries or responsibilities. Your response should be to rock, sing, and take care of the child, regardless of his or her age, as if the child were a baby.

Sometimes children "whine" to indicate that they need more undivided attention from their parents. They may be saying, "I want it to be like when I was a baby and you focused on me all the time." To help children who whine, add the I Love You Ritual called "Growing Up" (page 99) to your bedtime routine. If we meet the needs of our children on our terms, they have no need to demand attention inappropriately on their terms.

"I'm asleep": A child who plays this game may indicate one of two things. First, the child may be saying, "I feel comfortable and relaxed with you; safe enough just to nod off." Or the child may be trying to control the situation and may be communicating: "This situation is very frightening for me. I am scared it will not go the way I want it to go. This is too overwhelming for me. Will you go away if I go away?" The response is to stay engaged with the child. Do not leave the child. You may choose to rock and sing to the child. A child who pretends to sleep during inappropriate times is saying, "I am not getting the focused attention I need from you. I feel invisible. I want you to be present with me." Practice bringing your mind to where your body is and being present in the moment.

"Stealing" body parts: If the child begins to "steal" some of your body parts (as in the "I got your nose" game), it may be an indication that the child likes you enough to want to be a part of you. "Is it OK that I like you this much?" may be the message of the interaction. Your response is to play the game. You may say, "You got my nose. Where is my nose? I can't smell." You may then continue the game by stealing a child's body part and saying, "I got your ear. I can hear you talking in my head." Silliness and delight are the secrets of being in the moment with children.

Reaching out and touching an adult: When the child initiates touch with you, it is a statement that your relationship is highly valued. The child is feeling safe with you. Your response is to let the child know that you appreciate the contact. You can do so verbally and nonverbally. You may say, "You walked over and touched my hair. I really liked that." Your acknowledgment of the child's actions helps the child become aware of herself or himself. When we become aware of ourselves, we increase our self-control. These statements are therefore important in helping your child develop emotional intelligence.

Playing oldies but goodies: When children bring up past games to play, they are saying, "I care about what we have done together. Our time of play is important to me, and I remember it well. I have had fun, and I want it to continue." Your response is to be willing and receptive to the children's suggestions. You might say, "I remember that game too," or "I enjoyed playing that game with you also. At bedtime we can do it again."

USING I LOVE YOU RITUALS TO HELP CHILDREN UNDER STRESS

The brain is hard-wired to survive. As an infant you learned the fastest those things that you needed for survival, such as eating, talking, and walking. The brain stem is the part of your brain that directs your behavior under negative stress. Negative stress is stress over which you feel you have no control. If, in a family of four, Dad is transferred to a job in another city, it may produce different types of stress for the family members. If Dad gets a promotion and is excited about his new job, he will be exposed to minimum or moderate stress. This stress will be motivating for him. If Mom feels as if she has been forced to quit a job she loves with no possibility of employment in the new location, her stress is negative. If the youngest child is under three, she will sense all the emotions of the parents and will feel overwhelmed. If the older child is eleven and thinks he is leaving his best friends for life, the stress is negative. Stress is situation specific and can be positive or negative, depending on your perceptions and developmental level.

Negative stress first causes the body to release adrenaline into the bloodstream, which immediately increases your heart rate, depresses your immune system, and gets your body ready for flight-or-fight responses. The brain goes into survival mode. It becomes less capable of planning, receiving information, problem solving or performing any higher-order thinking skills. In other words, we become defensive, resisting comfort from others, perhaps complaining and whining. We reduce eye contact and our overall connection with others. We may shut out others or fight them tooth and nail. We may adopt an attitude of "I'll show you!" or "why bother?" or "why try?"

After about five minutes, the adrenal glands release another substance called cortisol in the hope of reestablishing balance in the body. Cortisol's job is to vacuum up the leftover adrenaline when the stress is over. It is designed to stay in the bloodstream only for short periods. If the stress continues, however, cortisol lingers, frantically attempting to remove the excess adrenalin. At this point, cortisol becomes devastating to the brain. It goes to an area of your brain called the hippocampus and has the capacity to kill brain cells. The area of the brain being destroyed is the part necessary for learning, memory, and emotion. Elderly patients with Alzheimer's disease have significantly smaller hippocampuses than do other adults.

So stress affects us on a continuum. A little stress is often motivating. Slightly more stress is tolerable with help and support from loved ones who constantly reassure us that all is well. Moderate stress impairs our ability to get along with others, and chronic stress disconnects us from each other and significantly impairs our ability to be empathic and to solve problems.

The main difference between conducting I Love You Rituals with children who are facing stress and children with few stressors in their lives is the way they respond to the games. Children who are feeling fairly secure with themselves and their world enjoy the I Love You Rituals. They will respond to your initiations with delight. Children who are under a minimal amount of stress will actively seek more and more of the I Love You Rituals, for the games "turn off" the stress response in the body. You will hear, "do it again," over and over. Children who are overwhelmed or chronically stressed may resist the games at first or give you no clue that they are having fun. I have found that I Love You Rituals are wonderful for all young children, but they are especially helpful for children who are experiencing challenges.

Stress for a four year old is different from stress for an adult. Not being invited to a friend's birthday party, not getting to color when you want to, or having to go to bed without watching a favorite video can add up to a bad day for a preschooler. Children roughly fifteen months to three years of age are under stress simply because of the developmental issues they are working to resolve. They are moving from dependence to independence in many areas and are beginning toilet training. I Love You Rituals are essential to help all parties successfully maneuver through the "terrible twos."

I LOVE YOU RITUALS AND CHILDREN WHO HAVE EXPERIENCED SEVERE, CHRONIC STRESS

I Love You Rituals are essential for teachers, caregivers, or parents of children who have experienced a great deal of pain in their lives. Children who are hurting are at risk of becoming children who hate. Children who are hurting are wonderful, but something sad or hurtful has happened in their lives. They are anxious and frightened. They have lost trust in adults; perhaps they have never experienced trust. Without a trusting relationship, children lose faith in themselves, others, and the world, becoming locked in self-defeating attitudes and actions. These children may be angry, antagonistic, withdrawn, or defensive. Individually, they can be a handful to deal with, and in group settings (such as child care or school), their behaviors challenge even the best educator.

Often children who are experiencing chronic stress have lost someone with whom they had a close bond. Stressful situations—divorce, death, unhappy or tense marriages, adoption, moving from school to school, medical issues (such as chronic ear infections, premature births, hospitalizations, and accidents), suicide of a parent, and poverty—all convey the message that life is unsafe. Some family relationships are strongly infected with rejection, criticisms, violence, and neglect. When the world seems overwhelming to children, they assume that no one cares for them. They internalize their overwhelming feelings and decide that adults and the world are not to be trusted. Children who hurt come from all walks of life. Their inappropriate behaviors are pleas for unqualified acceptance and love, as well as for appropriate guidance.

The good news is that young children who have experienced chronic stress can heal. The healing will not come through words or specific disciplinary actions, but through the relationship you establish with them. Many of these children have not experienced healthy bonded relationships with an adult. They fight being connected with others. Their goal is to control, not to engage with others. They resist parents' attempts to set limits and nurture them. Therefore, their relationship with authority is unhealthy and will continue to be so unless an adult intervenes. Children who have experienced chronic stress need an adult who is willing to make a commitment to them. To help these children heal from their hurts, a caring adult needs to build a relationship based on acceptance and love. If you have ever lived in an area that experienced a drought, you noticed that the grass turns brown and stops growing. When you pour water on dry ground, the earth resists the water it so desperately needs. The water beads up almost as if it were drops of oil, but if you continue to flood the area, the earth's resistance recedes and the water is absorbed. Children who hurt are suffering an emotional drought. They may resist the first love you offer them. Their resistance may be verbal ("This is for babies") or physical (looking away, moving away, or pretending to fall asleep). As we flood them with our persistent commitment to their beauty, their resistance ceases and our love is accepted. The ultimate task is to establish and develop a relationship built on acceptance. This relationship will enable children to change their view of themselves and ultimately their view of the world, which will lead to changes in their behavior.

I believe that these activities are essential for young children who have experienced chronic stress to interact successfully in group settings, such as schools. Children who have experienced minimum stress see other children as possible friends. Children who have experienced chronic stress are overwhelmed. They believe there is not enough love, time, money, or other resources to go around. They see other children as competitors for scarce resources and tend to fight with them, rather than cooperate.

Not all children have experienced chronic stress and significant life challenges, but the numbers are increasing. If you have time, become a volunteer. Take this book to your local schools and get involved. Tutor young children by reading to them and end your time together with an I Love You Ritual. Your contribution to humanity will be greatly appreciated.

Elements to Remember When Playing with Children Who Have Experienced Challenges

1. The adult is in charge. The adult is the leader in these games. These games are modeled after parent-infant interactions and require the partners to engage in a dance, with the adult leading. It would seem silly for a parent to look at her four-month-old baby and ask, "What will we play?" or "How will we play this game?" The adult initiates the interactions and continues with delight as long as the interaction is sustained. Being in charge requires the adult to stay engaged with the child, regardless of the child's response. Use the responses modeled in the section of this chapter on Learning the Language of Young Children to help you remain in charge.

2. Have fun. Each activity, whether the child resists or not, is surrounded by playfulness and fun. When an infant struggles as you are trying to dress him or her, a responsible parent tries to make a game out of it by singing, tickling, soothing, or making sounds in time with the movement. Getting angry at the infant's resistance to getting dressed does nothing but weaken the infant's trust in the safety of the relationship. The same is true for these I Love You Rituals. Some children may resist having fun. The role of the adult is to coax them out of their control and into engagement by continuing to be playful, regardless of the children's responses. Children who have experienced challenges in life may turn many of the interactions into hide-and-seek or peek-a-boo games. As was mentioned earlier, they need to ask the symbolic question, "Do you care enough to go looking for me?" or "If I go away, will you leave me?" many, many times to feel reassured. They need to hear your symbolic answer, "I will find you; I will not

leave you" over and over again. This is especially true for some children who are adopted.

3. No hurts. The adult, while in charge, must create an atmosphere of safety and nurturance. The games require a caring, gentle touch. No hitting or hurts of any kind are allowed. If the child strikes out at you, stop the hit if possible and state, "No hurts. I will not hurt you, and I will not let you hurt me." Once the limit is stated, continue with the game.

4. Stick together. Keep close to the child. These interactions are intimate, loving games. Sometimes you may think, "This child could do this without me. I will just teach her how to do the finger plays." The goal of I Love You Rituals is not to teach the child to say the rhyme, do the motions, or sing the song. The goal is to create a connection between the two of you.

5. Touch children firmly. With one of your hands, firmly and gently grasp your other forearm. Remove your hand. Can you still feel a lingering presence of where your hand used to be? That is about the firmness you will want to use. Remember to be sensitive to the child's cues. This type of touch releases the nerve growth hormone in the body mentioned in chapter one.

6. Do not tickle. Tickling can easily cross the line between fun and a form of aggression. Many of us experienced this phenomenon when we were children. Children who have experienced challenges may misperceive tickling. Pay attention to their cues. "Stop" means stop, even if they are laughing.

7. Do not give up on the child. Some children who have experienced severe challenges early in life may be resistant to the games at first. Continue to be playful and caring. Do not let the child's response push you away. If you decided to run a marathon, would you jog fifteen miles tomorrow? Probably not. You would need to start slowly, maybe just by walking to the mailbox and back. Some children need us to start slowly and to be persistent and consistent. You know your child. These games are fun. Sometimes we need only to move through the walls of defensiveness enough to let the trapped joy out.

A second-grade teacher shared a story that involved her and a child in her classroom who had experienced a great deal of pain and challenge in his young life. Gary had entered public school as a kindergartner. He immediately was labeled as a child with problems. During his first two years of school, Gary was diagnosed but not helped. His behavior and academic skills continued to worsen as time went on. When he entered the second grade, his teacher decided to make a commitment to establishing a relationship with him. *Every* morning when Gary arrived at school, his teacher would take Gary's head gently between her two hands and touch her forehead to his and say, "I am so glad to see you and so glad you are in my class." Gary would withdraw from the touch, mumble under his breath, and shrug his shoulders as if he did not care about the greeting, the touch, or the teacher. Nevertheless, Gary's schoolwork improved that year, and he began reading despite the challenges he faced at home. The teacher continued this I Love You Ritual for 179 days of the 180-day school year. Each day Gary did not show one sign that this ritual had meaning for him or that he cared whether it occurred or not. The teacher, committed to Gary, persisted in her desire to reach him. On the final day of school, she was preoccupied with the class goodbye party and forgot to greet Gary. For the first time in Gary's school life, he sought out another person, initiated contact, and spoke. He walked over and leaned against the teacher. He stroked her hair and said, "You forgot our thing this morning." Gary and his teacher had both been touched literally and figuratively. These small moments, unconditionally given by the adult to the child, changed both their lives.

CREATING RITUALS: CARVING OUT SACRED SPACES

Rituals are love moments. They are the moments in life when all else stops, and we take time to reconnect with each other and remember who we are—loving, caring beings. Rituals can serve us well during transitions during a busy day. The transition from sleeping to waking is a wonderful time for a ritual. I remember my parents waking my brother and me up by turning on the light and loudly saying, "Time to get up." I thought all families did it this way until I slept over at a friend's house, where her mom would come into the bedroom and stroke my friend's head and say, "Wake up those sleepy eyes." What a delight, I thought. I asked if this was done every morning or just on Saturdays. She said, "Oh that, Mom does it every morning. My brother hates it." Her brother is now thirty-eight years old and wakes his children up the same way. His mother has sinced passed away. I once asked him about the ritual. He said with tears in his eyes, "That is what I remember most about my mom, how she would stroke my head. I can still hear her saying, "Wake up those sleepy eyes."

Here are some suggested times for rituals:

1. When your children wake up
2. When your children go to bed
3. When you send your children to and welcome them home from school
4. When you or your children leave or return from a trip
5. At other "Hello" and "Good-bye" times
6. During "life change" times, such as a birthday, getting a new tooth, losing a tooth, graduation, the birth of a new sibling, and so on.
7. During family time, healing time, or any other time together

Using the Power of Rituals

Rituals are the lenses through which we see our emotional connections to each other, to a culture, and to a higher power. They are symbolic expressions of our most sacred values.

Every year when a birthday is celebrated, some form of ritual usually marks the event. Some families may have traditional birthday cakes while others observe the event differently. Rituals ground us. The familiarity and predictability of rituals provides safety as well as excitement; for example, birthday presents are predicted, yet they are wrapped.

According to Drs. Evan Imber-Black and Janine Roberts, in their insightful 1992 book *Rituals for Our Times*, rituals serve five purposes in our lives: relating, changing, healing, celebrating, and believing. Using these purposes as guideposts, here are some ideas for using specific I Love You Rituals to unite your family.

1. Relating. Rituals shape, express, and maintain relationships. They have the power to preserve human ties during intense turmoil. My grandmother and I used to sit on the couch in a special way and snap beans together. It was an unspoken I Love You Ritual we developed during my childhood. Once when I visited her during my spring break from college, I woke up early to find her sitting in a chair, clutching her chest with pain. She had angina, and in those days there was little that doctors could do for this painful heart condition. When I saw my grandmother in pain, I was frightened. She looked in deep distress. Our eyes met with a special knowledge and she said, "Get the beans. We might as well get an early start on this day." My fears subsided. Our connection was solid, and for that moment all was well. The bean-snapping ritual cocooned us in our shared love.

   Although every I Love You Ritual in this book is designed to build relationships, the interactive finger plays in Chapter 5 are specifically configured to enhance relating. They will help you shape, express, and maintain your relationship with your children or grandchildren.

2. Changing. Rituals mark transitions in life. The change is enacted through the ritual, not just talked about. It is one thing to have a loose tooth, to wriggle it, and then for it to fall out. It is another thing to mark the transition with a tooth-fairy ritual. In our rapidly changing society, rituals are essential for marking transitions. Many of our children, as well as adults, are overwhelmed with change. Both mothers and fathers must shift from being workers during the day to parents and spouses in the evening. These transitions can be rough if rituals are not embedded in family life.

   Here are some I Love You Rituals that you may want to use to mark transitions in your household:

Bedtime/Waking Rituals   **Page**

This Little Finger Goes Night-Night   122

Your Fingers Are So Sleepy   133

Goodnight Elbow   155

Hello, Toes/Good-bye, Toes   175

Held in My Arms   194

Growing Milestones

Growing Up (birth of a new sibling)   99

Guess What I Am Writing [Drawing]? (getting smarter) 156

Story Hand   167

Going to or Returning from School

What Did You Bring Home from School Today?   145

This Little Finger   119

Mama's Smart Girl [Boy]   152

Dressing/Undressing

Jelly Bean Toes   149

Silly Me   148

Hello, Toes/Good-bye, Toes   175

Where Are Those Hands?   181

Where Did It Go?   183

Hello/Good-bye

On Your Face   107

The Hello Game   117

I Love You
Rituals

54

You've Been Gone	136
Greetings	144
Find the Stickers	171
Find the Yarn	173
Family Handshakes	141
This Little Finger	119

3. Healing. In every relationship there are stressful times when healing is needed. This is true for adults and for children. Significant loss through death, divorce, and/or a move can all leave psychological wounds. Through loss, betrayal, and hurt children can lose trust in the world. "Will someone be there for me?" is their main question. Young children do not ask this question aloud; they do not have the cognitive or language skills to formulate the concept. They ask through their behavior, usually through their misbehavior. As noted earlier, they may ask this question by running off to see if you will come after them or by playing a variety of hide-and-seek maneuvers. These are usually played at inappropriate times and can create dangerous situations. Therefore, Chapter 8 contains hide-and-seek games you can initiate with your child. Either you initiate the game in your house on your terms, or children will initiate the game in the grocery store. In addition to hide-and-seek games, the following games are very healing for children who have experienced a number of life's challenges.

I Love You Ritual	Page
Humpty Dumpty	67
Putting Lotion on the Hurts	160
The Big Crash	201
Row, Row, Row Your Boat	190
Twinkle, Twinkle, Little Star	63

Some children who are overwhelmed by life become grumpy and resistant. This is certainly true of toddlers who feel conflicted as they battle dependence and independence issues. The following I Love You Rituals are helpful with grumpy children.

I Love You Ritual	Page
Yes and No Game	150
My Hand Is Stuck	143
Snuggle Up	192
Jack Be Noodle	85
Three Nice Mice	89

4. Celebrating. All cultures have celebrations. We celebrate birthdays, weddings, and holidays. Celebration is one of the most universal forms of ritual. Every ritual in this book is a celebration of the adult, the child, and their connection to each other. Specifically, you may want to add some of the following birthday and holiday I Love You Rituals to your child's life experiences:

I Love You Ritual	Page
Today Is _____'s Birthday	123
Ten Little Candles	114
You Have a Present	151

5. Believing. Rituals are the deepest expression of our most cherished values. They pass a culture from one generation to the next. Every time we participate in a ritual, we are expressing our beliefs and passing them on. Chapter 4 contains interactive, positive nursery rhymes. These nursery rhymes have been changed from the original verses written in the fifteenth century to express the culture of caring and respect.

Start using the power of I Love You Rituals today. Open the book to any page. It will be the perfect one for you and your child. Have fun!

Chapter
4

Positive Nursery Rhymes

If we don't change our direction, we
are likely to end up where we are headed.

—Ancient Chinese proverb

A Wonderful Woman
Who Lived in a Shoe

A wonderful woman lived in a shoe.

She had so many children

She knew exactly what to do.

She held them,

She rocked them,

And tucked them in bed.

"I love you, I love you,"

Is what she said.

Preparation and Instructions:
This is a wonderful poem to share with your children at naptime or bedtime. Have the child sit in your lap or lean against your body. Wrap your arms around the child and hold on to one hand.

"A wonderful woman lived in a shoe."

As you say this line, turn the child's hands so they are facing you, palms out. As you say the next line, give the child's hand a nice, deep hand massage.

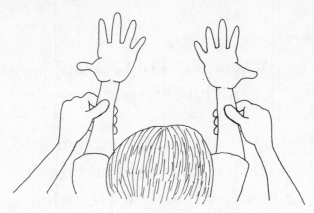

"She had so many children"

Touch each finger on one hand as you say each word in this line.

"She knew exactly what to do."

Begin touching the fingers of the other hand. Since there are six words in this line, say one word per finger except for "to do." Say these two words together as you touch the last finger.

"She held them,"

Fold your child's fingers into a fist and put both your hands around the child's hand, as though you are swaddling the child's hand in your hands.

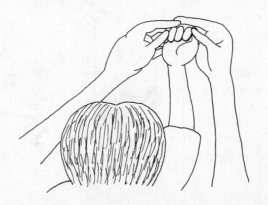

"She rocked them,"

Holding the child's hand securely, rock it from side to side.

"And tucked them in bed."

Press the child's hand against his or her chest. This will place
you in a slight hugging position.

"I love you, I love you," is what she said.

Say these words lovingly to the child and give the child a hug.

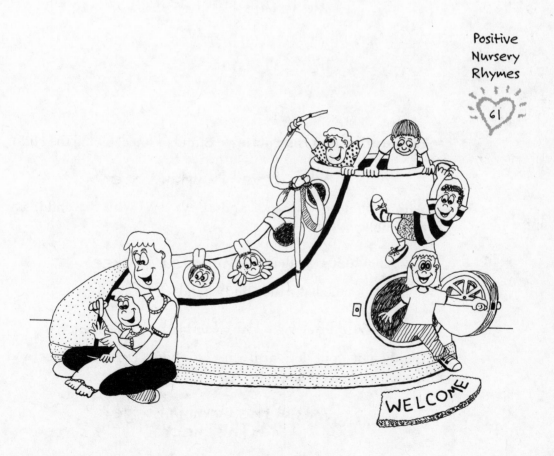

WELCOME

Peter, Peter, Pumpkin Eater

Peter, Peter, Pumpkin Eater,
Had a friend he loved to greet.
Treated her [him] with kind respect,
And in the morning hugged
her [his] neck.

Preparation and Instructions: Stand or kneel facing the child.

"Peter, Peter, Pumpkin Eater,"

With delight on your face and at eye level with the child, say this line.

"Had a friend he loved to greet."

Reach out and shake the child's hand.

"Treated her [him] with kind respect,"

Gently put your left arm on the child's right shoulder and demonstrate a kind touch.

"And in the morning hugged her [his] neck."

Move from this position into a gentle hug.

Twinkle, Twinkle, Little Star

Twinkle, twinkle, little star,
What a wonderful child you are!
With bright eyes and nice
round cheeks,
Talented person from head to feet.
Twinkle, twinkle, little star,
What a wonderful child you are!

Preparation and Instructions: It is important that you be at the same height as the child for this activity. You may choose to stand, kneel, or sit with the child to attain this position.

"Twinkle, twinkle, little star,"

Hold your child's hands and raise them slightly above your heads. Wiggle your fingers together to represent the "twinkle" of stars.

"What a wonderful child you are!"

Bring your arms down and rest your hands on your child's shoulders with the child's hands on your shoulders.

"With bright eyes and nice round cheeks,"

Take your hands off the child's shoulders and touch the child's face with your index fingers. First, touch the child next to his eyes. Then draw your fingers down around the child's cheeks.

"Talented person from head to feet."

Take the child's hands in yours and swing them up high (above the child's head) and sweep them down low (to the child's feet).

"Twinkle, twinkle, little star,"

Raise the child's hands and touch fingertips as in the beginning. Wiggle your fingertips to represent the shining stars.

"What a wonderful child you are!"

End the interaction with a hug.

Little Miss Muffet

Little Miss Muffet sat on her tuffet,
Eating her oatmeal today.
Along came a spider and sat down
beside her,
And said, "Have a good day!"

Preparation and Instructions: Explain to the child that a tuffet is a little chair. Both you and the child will each make a tuffet by making a fist with your hands. Place your tuffets together with knuckles touching. Tell the child that you will be Miss Muffet and the child will be the spider.

"Little Miss Muffet sat on her tuffet,"

With your nontuffet hand, make little Miss Muffet by holding up two bent fingers from a fist. While saying these words, bring Miss Muffet over and have her sit on your other hand, or tuffet.

"Eating her oatmeal today."

Move your two upright fingers back and forth in an eating motion.

"Along came a spider and sat down beside her,"

The child will use his nontuffet hand as a spider. Holding the hand palm down with fingers dangling like the legs of a spider, the child is to "walk" the spider over to sit on the tuffet hand.

And said, "Have a good day!"

Use your Little Miss Muffet hand to open the child's tuffet hand and shake that hand while lovingly saying, "Have a good day!"

Humpty Dumpty

Humpty Dumpty sat on the wall.
Humpty Dumpty had a great fall.
All the Queen's horses and
All the King's men,
Could put Humpty together again.

Preparation and Instructions: In this game, your hands make the wall and the child's hands make Humpty Dumpty. The message is, "I will support you." Create the wall by holding your hands out in front of you, palms facing your body and thumbs pointing up and extended 90 degrees from the fingers. The fingertips of each hand should be touching. The two Humpty Dumptys are made by the child closing both hands into fists.

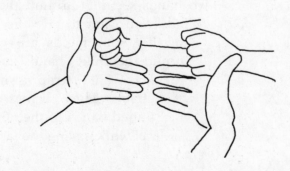

"Humpty Dumpty sat on the wall."

Hold up your "wall" and have the child place her or his two fists on top of the wall. Say the first line of the rhyme.

"Humpty Dumpty had a great fall."

Gently grasp the child's arms (at about wrist level) as the two Humpty Dumptys fall down to each side of the child. (It is important to hold onto the child at all times, sending the message, "You have fallen, but I am here to catch you.")

"All the Queen's horses and"

While saying this line, release the child's wrists, move your hands up the child's arms just below the elbow, and give the child's arms a gentle, yet firm forearm massage.

"All the King's men"

Continue the massage action.

"Could put Humpty together again."

Bring the child's hands together so that one of the child's fists wraps around the other fist. Then wrap your two hands securely around the child's hands. You want to give the impression that your hands are wrapped around the child's hands as a blanket would wrap a newborn baby. Then bring all the united hands to the child's eye level while saying the last line.

Georgie Porgie

Georgie Porgie, pudding and pie,
Gave his friend a big high five!
With his friend he loved to play,
A gift of a smile he gave each day.

Preparation and Instructions: This poem gives you the opportunity to expand the concept of gifts with children. True gifts are the love we share with each other, not material goods. Children learn that a smile is a gift of joy to be treasured. As you expand on this rhyme, you can ask the children for other "gifts" that can be given, such as a hug or a wink, and include them in the poem. Other possible gifts are pinky hugs (little fingers intertwined), thumb touches, and a kiss (blow a kiss). Stand or sit facing each other to begin this I Love You ritual.

"Georgie Porgie, pudding and pie,"

Move your shoulders up and down to the rhythm of the words.

"Gave his friend a big high five!"

With both hands, execute a loving, gentle high five with the child.

"With his friend he loved to play,"

Holding your hands in front of you with your fingers pointing up and palms facing the child, wiggle your fingers with delight and touch the wiggling fingers of the child. This is a fast, happy motion as if you were tickling each other's fingers in the air. Be sure to make contact with the child's fingertips while making this delightful motion.

"A gift of a smile he gave each day."

With a big smile, put your hands up to your face and, in essence, use your hands to "blow" a smile to the child.

I Love You
Rituals

70

Margie Pargie

Margie Pargie, pudding and pie,
Gave her friend a big high five!
With her friend she loved to play,
A gift of handshake she gave
each day.

Preparation and Instructions: Margie Pargie is conducted in the same manner as Georgie Porgie, but the gift given at the end is a friendly handshake.

Mary Had a Little Lamb

Mary had a little lamb
whose fleece was white as snow.
Everywhere that Mary went
the lamb was sure to go.
It followed her to school one day;
everything was new.
The children were surprised to see
the lamb was really you!

Preparation and Instructions: You will need a white sock for this game. Introduce yourself as Mary before you begin the rhyme by waving hello and saying, "Hello, it is wonderful to see you. My name is Mary. I am looking for a lamb to play with. I think I see one!" (look directly at one of the child's hands). Now you are ready to begin the rhyme.

"Mary had a little lamb whose fleece was white as snow."

While saying this line, put the white sock on one of the child's hands.

"Everywhere that Mary went the lamb was sure to go."

Put the hand that you introduced as Mary on the lamb (the child's hand covered with the sock). Move both hands around, making sure they are always touching.

"It followed her to school one day; everything was new."

Continue to move both hands up and down and all around in this mirror-play fashion.

"The children were surprised to see the lamb was really you!"

Pull the sock off the child's hand and look surprised and delighted.

Message of the Game: The message of this game is, "I will be with you no matter what happens. I am here for you." Many children will test to see if you really mean what you say. They will do so by making it difficult for your hand to stay in contact with theirs. Some children will hide their hands or run away to begin a game of hide-and-seek. If the child gets away from you, begin the Little Bo Peep rhyme (presented next). The two games played together are delightful.

Little Bo Peep

Little Bo Peep has lost her sheep
And doesn't know where to find
them.
She'll look for them and bring them
home
Staying always close beside them.

Preparation and Instructions: This game can be played by itself or as an extension of Mary Had a Little Lamb (see page 72).

"Little Bo Peep has lost her sheep"

As you say this line in a sad voice, have your hands begin to "look for" your child's hands. If you are playing this game as an extension of Mary Had a Little Lamb, more than likely the child is hiding his or her hands or has run away from you, so you will need to search for the child's hands. If your child's hands are not hidden, you can look at one of them as you say this line.

"And doesn't know where to find them."

Make an exaggerated facial expression that displays confusion and sadness. Then make a questioning face as if to say, "Where could they be?" If your child has run off or continues to hide his or her hands, you can become very sad. You may want to repeat this line and pretend to begin to cry. This sends a message to the child, "I feel sad. I miss you. I hope your hands come back to play."

"She'll look for them and bring them home"

Look all around for the child's hands, especially in silly places (whether they are still hidden or not). Look in the child's ears, inside a sleeve, and in a sock or shoe.

"Staying always close beside them."

Once you find the child's hands, give the child a loving hug. If the child continues to hide his or her hands, simply end the rhyme with your hands near the child's hands.

Hot Cross Buns

Hot cross buns, hot cross buns.

One penny, two penny

Hot cross buns!

Give them to your daughters;

give them to your sons.

One penny, two penny

Hot cross buns!

Preparation and Instructions: This ritual entails slightly more difficult hand motions than the previous games. Young children (3–5 years) will be more successful if you teach the hand-clapping sequence first without any words. Once they have mastered the clapping, you are ready for words and actions. Older children will have no trouble learning the words and actions simultaneously.

Sit facing the child. Give the child a signal to begin the game by saying, "Ready, set, go!"

"Hot cross buns, hot cross buns."

Each clap is made in time with the words. When you say, "Hot," clap your thighs with both hands. When you say, "Cross," clap your hands together, and when you say, "Buns," clap the child's hands. The child is to mirror your actions.

"One penny, two penny"

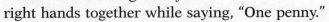

Both you and the child will hold up the index fingers of your right hands and two fingers (index and middle fingers) of their left hands. You and the child touch the index finger on your right hands together while saying, "One penny." Next, touch the two fingers of the left hands together and say, "Two penny." Your hand will cross the midline of your body to reach your child. This crossing-over process is an excellent brain-boosting maneuver.

"Hot cross buns!"

Repeat the hand-clapping pattern that you began with.

"Give them to your daughters; give them to your sons."

When you say, "Give them to your daughters," use your right hand to shake the child's right hand. When you say, "give them to your sons," use your left hand to shake the child's left hand. Again, this process of crossing the center of your body is important for your child's development because it helps to integrate the child's brain hemispheres.

"One penny, two penny"

Repeat the finger touches as before.

"Hot cross buns!"

End the interaction with a final series of hand claps as you did before. To review:

"**Hot**"—clap your thighs

"**cross**"—clap your hands together

"**buns**"—clap the child's hands

Mary, Mary, Extraordinary

Mary, Mary [Jerry, Jerry],
Extraordinary,
How do your fingers grow?
With fingernails and no tails,
And a high five to go.

Preparation and Instructions: Facing your child, have the child ball his or her hands into fists. Then do the same. Both of you extend your fists, touching each other.

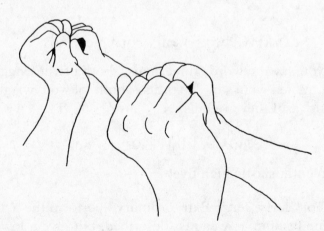

"Mary, Mary [Jerry, Jerry], Extraordinary,"

Stand with your fists touching as was just indicated. You may use either the female or the male name for the game.

"How do your fingers grow?"

As you say this line, you and the child should make your fingers spring up from a closed-fist position to an extended, open position. Now the palms of your hands are touching the child's palms.

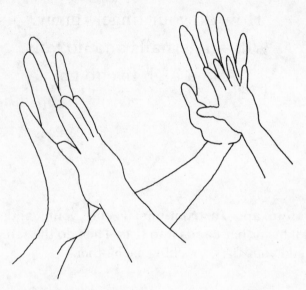

"With fingernails and no tails,"

When you say the word "fingernails," both of you wiggle your fingers. When you say "no tails," both of you wiggle your "behinds" as if they are tails.

"And a high five to go."

Give an enthusiastic high five!

Note: For "Jerry, Jerry, Extraordinary," perform the activity in the same fashion as was just described, but give a low five at the end.

To Market, to Market

To market, to market, to buy a
fat pig.
Home again, home again, jiggity jig.
To market, to market, to buy a
fat hog.
Home again, home again, jiggity jog.
To market, to market, to buy a
new gown.
Home again, home again—
Whoops! the horse fell down.

Preparation and Instructions: This is a game with an element of risk (falling or being hurt). Its underlying message is, "I am here to keep you safe." Children who have been through some recent challenges may find the game anxiety producing. In their anxiety, they may respond in a number of ways. Some children may try to make the game rougher and more dangerous, actually creating a situation in which you may find it hard to hold onto them and keep them safe. Some children may become limp like a noodle. Others may go along with the game, but may appear to take no joy in the activity. Play this game gently with impulsive children who have a tendency to fly off the handle. You control the pace and the roughness of the horse—do not let the child do so. Start the game by having the child say, "Giddyap!" This lets the child control when the movement will begin and helps to reduce anxiety.

"To market, to market, to buy a fat pig.

Home again, home again, jiggity jig."

Have the child sit on your lap facing you with his or her legs straddling your legs. Gently bounce the child as if he or she is riding a pony to the market while holding both of the child's hands.

"To market, to market, to buy a fat hog.

Home again, home again, jiggity jog."

Repeat the action. Vary the intensity, depending on the child (see the instructions).

"To market, to market, to buy a new gown.

Home again, home again—"

Continue with the horsey ride, holding onto both the child's hands with a firm grip.

"Whoops! The horse fell down."

Spread your legs and let the child fall gently through your legs as you support and catch him or her.

Wee Willie [Wendy] Winkie

Wee Willy [Wendy] Winkie
runs through the town.
Upstairs and downstairs
in his [her] nightgown.
Rapping at the window,
Looking through the lock.
"Are the children in their beds,
For now it's eight o'clock?"

Preparation and Instructions: The final lines of this poem give you many opportunities. You can vary the time to mesh with your schedule. At times, you may want to change the question entirely. You could say, "Are the children eating breakfast, for now it's seven o'clock?" This is an excellent alternative to shouting commands over and over. If it is time to go to bed, eat breakfast, or get in the car, Wee Willie Winkie is a helpful game.

"Wee Willy [Wendy] Winkie runs through the town."

Holding the palm of the child's hand in yours, place two fingers of your other hand on the child's palm. Move your two fingers up and down on the child's palm as if they are warming up to run in a race.

"Upstairs and downstairs in his [her] nightgown."

When you say "upstairs," run your two fingers up to the child's elbow. When you say "downstairs," run them back down to the child's palm. When you say, "in his [her] nightgown," look surprised.

"Rapping at the window,"

Make each hand into a fist as if you are knocking on a door and gently tap the child on each side of his or her head four times.

"Looking through the lock."

Cover the child's eyes with your hands as if to play peek-a-boo. Then move aside your hands to see the child. As you move your hands, move up close to peek at the child's face.

"Are the children in their beds,"

With your hands cupped at the child's temples; your head close to the child's face; and a stern, curious facial expression ask, "Are the children in their beds?"

"For now it's eight o'clock?"

Remove your hands and point to your wristwatch. If you do not have a watch, point to a clock on the wall or counter.

Jack Be Noodle

Jack be noodle,
Jack be stiff,
Jack come over and hug me quick.

Preparation and Instructions: You can perform Jack Be Noodle three times, focusing on three different body parts. For example, begin with the child's index finger, then use the whole hand, and finish using the child's entire arm.

"Jack be noodle,"

Stand or kneel facing the child and hold her or his index finger. As you say "Jack be noodle," wriggle the child's finger as if to make it loose and floppy.

"Jack be stiff,"

When you say these words, move your fingers over the child's finger to make it stiff.

"Jack come over and hug me quick."

Lock your index finger with the child's finger as if to do a finger hug.

"Jack be Noodle"

Repeat these actions using the child's entire hand. Hold the child's wrist and make the child's hand be floppy.

"Jack be stiff,"

This time help the child make a stiff hand.

"Jack come over and hug me quick."

Exchange a handshake.

"Jack be noodle,"

Repeat these actions and words making the child's entire arm floppy from the shoulder down.

"Jack be stiff,"

Help the child make a stiff arm.

"Jack come over and hug me quick."

Give the child a hug.

Ba Ba, Black Sheep

Ba Ba, black sheep. Have you any
wool?
Yes ma'am, yes ma'am, three bags
full.
One for mittens, one for a cap.
And one for the little boy [girl]
who sits in my lap.

Preparation and Instructions: This is a wonderful game to play when you want to get hold of your toddler to put on his or her shoes or to hasten the dressing process. It is also a delightful precursor for slightly older children (3–5 years) to signal "cuddle time."

"Ba ba, black sheep. Have you any wool?"

As you say this line, raise your shoulders and open your hands as if you are asking a question.

"Yes ma'am, yes ma'am, three bags full."

Hold up three fingers as you say "three bags full."

"One for mittens, one for a cap."

Cover one of the child's hands with both of yours as if you are putting on mittens. Then place both your hands on the child's head as if you are putting on a cap.

"And one for the little boy [girl] who sits in my lap."

Pick your child up and place him or her in your lap. Then hug and squeeze your child to show your delight.

Variations: The last line can be changed to, "And one for the little boy [or girl] with hands in his [or her] lap." This rhyme can be used at dinner or with a group of children to help them sit close to each other and keep their hands to themselves.

Three Nice Mice

Three nice mice. Three nice mice.

See how they care.

See how they care.

They hold both hands

and give a shake.

Smiling together, good friends

they make.

Then turning around,

for goodness' sake.

Three nice mice. Three nice mice.

Preparation and Instructions: This is a wonderful rhyme to teach children to do with each other. Older siblings will enjoy teaching this fun interaction to their younger brothers and sisters.

"Three nice mice. Three nice mice."

As you say each sentence, hold up three fingers on each hand. Have the child mirror your actions and hold up three fingers also.

"See how they care. See how they care."

You and the child form circles with both your right and left hands. Then you both bring the circles up to your eyes as if to look through binoculars at the mice.

"They hold both hands and give a shake."

Reach out and hold hands. Move your clasped hands up and down in a handshake.

"Smiling together, good friends they make."

Continue holding hands and swinging them slightly from side to side as you keep rhythm with the rhyme.

"Then turning around, for goodness' sake."

Release your hands while each of you makes a complete turn. When you are again face to face, give each other a gentle, loving high five while saying, "for goodness' sake."

"Three nice mice. Three nice mice."

Return to holding up three fingers on each hand.

Chapter
5

Interactive Finger Plays

Together we're better!

—Bev Bos

Dancing Hands

[Child's name]'s hands are up and
[Child's name]'s hands are down.
[Child's name]'s hands are dancing
All around the town.

Dancing on my knees,
Dancing on my feet,
Dancing on my shoulders,
And dancing on my cheeks [blow
raspberries*].

[Child's name]'s hands are up and
[Child's name]'s hands are down.
[Child's name]'s hands are dancing
All around the town.

Dancing on your knees,
Dancing on your feet,
Dancing on your shoulders,
And dancing on your cheeks [blow
raspberries*].

Interactive
Finger
Plays

93

---

*Blowing raspberries is an all-time favorite activity of children. To blow a raspberry, fill your cheeks with air, then gently touch them, forcing a squirt of air through your puckered lips.

Preparation and Instructions: This I Love You Ritual has two verses. For the first verse, move the child's hands and have him or her touch your body parts. For the second verse, move the child's hands and have the child touch himself or herself. Start by sitting together in a chair or on the floor.

"[Child's name]'s hands are up and"

Holding both your child's hands, raise his or her arms up high over the head.

"[Child's name]'s hands are down."

Bring both arms down.

"[Child's name]'s hands are dancing all around the town.

Move the child's hands around in the air.

"Dancing on my knees,"

Holding the child's hands, guide them to pat your knees.

"Dancing on my feet,"

Guide the child's hands to pat your feet.

"Dancing on my shoulders,"

Continue to your shoulders.

"And dancing on my cheeks."

As you bring the child's hands up to your face, fill your cheeks with air. Guide the child's hands to tap your cheeks gently so the air comes out in a "raspberry." This surprise ending is delightful to children.

Second Verse: The second verse is done the same way as the first, but this time you guide the child's hands to pat his or her own knees, feet, shoulders, and cheeks. Having seen you do it, it is to be hoped that the child will fill up his or her cheeks with air for the "raspberry" finale. You may have to help young children understand their role at the end.

Five Little Babies

One little baby
Rocking in a tree,
Two little babies
Looking at me.
Three little babies
Crawling on the floor,
Four little babies
Knocking on the door.
Five little babies
Playing hide-and-seek.
Don't look, don't look
Until I say . . . "PEEK!"

Preparation and Instructions: Sit with the child on your lap facing you or on the floor so you are face to face. Select one of the child's hands and have the child extend his or her fingers.

"One little baby"

Tap your index finger on the index finger of the child three times, in rhythm with the words.

"Rocking in a tree,"

Lay the child's hand across your cradled hands and rock the hand as if it were a baby doll.

"Two little babies"

Holding the child's hand, extend two of the child's fingers, tucking the rest into his or her palm.

"Looking at me."

Bring the child's two fingers close to your eyes as if they are pointing at your eyes.

"Three little babies"

Hold the child's hand so she or he is holding up three fingers.

"Crawling on the floor,"

Guide the child's fingers to move around on your thigh, representing a crawling action.

"Four little babies"

Hold the child's hand with four fingers extended.

"Knocking on the door."

Tap the child's four fingers gently on the side of your head. Simultaneously, make a knocking sound by clicking your tongue in your mouth twice.

"Five little babies"

Hold up both of the child's hands.

"Playing hide-and-seek."

Turn the child's hand to cover his or her eyes. The child may choose to peek through his or her hands.

"Don't look, don't look"

Keep holding the child's hands over his or her eyes, and bring your face slightly closer to the child's.

Until I say . . . "PEEK!"

When you say peek, assist the child in removing his hands from his eyes. Surprise the child with your smiling face.

I Love You
Rituals

98

Growing Up

When you were just a baby,
You did not know how to walk.
You could only crawl, crawl around
like this.
When you were just a baby,
You did not know how to talk.
You could only babble, babble just
like this.
Now you are this big.
And go to school each day.
You can do many things
Like walk and talk and play.

Preparation and Instructions: This is a wonderful activity for older siblings who are faced with a new baby in the family. They long for the time when they were the center of your focus. This game allows them to see themselves growing up while allowing them to reminisce about the "good old days." This is a poem that gives you the opportunity to hold your child. Place the child in your lap and hold him or her like a baby. In a soothing voice, share the poem with the child.

Variations: Children love to hear stories of when they were younger or when they were babies. This poem provides a perfect opportunity to share some of those cherished memories. It is also a wonderful time to share with the child all the things you have noticed she or he is capable of doing.

I Love You
Rituals

100

Here's the Beehive

Here's the beehive, where are the
bees?
Hidden away where nobody sees.
Watch and you will see them come
out of the hive.
One, two, three, four, five
Bzzzzzzzzzzzzzzzzzz
I'll catch them and keep them alive!

Preparation and Instructions: Start this game with the child making a fist with the thumb tucked inside his or her hand, so no "bees" are showing.

"Here's the beehive, where are the bees?"

Hold the child's closed fist and look all around the hand with an inquisitive expression.

"Hidden away where nobody sees."

Say this line with a sighing voice as you shrug your shoulders, looking at the child's closed hand.

"Watch and you will see them come out of the hive."

Showing anticipation and delight, prepare your other hand to "remove the bees."

"One, two, three, four, five"

Pick out one "bee" at a time as you count the child's fingers being opened. As each finger is extended, make the "Bzzzzz" sound.

"Bzzzzzzzz"

Once all the "bees" are out, continue making a bee sound and move the child's hand in a fluttering motion.

"I'll catch them and keep them alive!"

Pretend to catch the bees by gently tucking the child's fingers inside your hands. When the "bees" are caught, stop the buzzing noise. Check on the "bees" several times to make sure they are still alive by opening your hands and looking at them. Each time you check, show the child that the bees are alive by making a "Bzzzzz" noise.

Here's the Bunny

Here's the bunny with the ears so
funny.
Here's the hole in the ground.
When a noise she hears,
She picks up her ears,
And jumps in the hole in the ground!

Preparation and Instructions: In this game, the child is the bunny and the adult is the hole. The roles may change as the child becomes familiar with the game. The game can be played with the hands or with the whole body. When playing the game with the hands, the child makes a bunny by holding up two fingers of one hand. The adult makes the hole by configuring her or his hands as shown in the picture. When using the entire body, the child makes the bunny by extending his or her arms above the head to represent big ears on the bunny body. The hole is made by extending both your arms perpendicular to the floor and linking your fingers to form a circle.

"Here's the bunny with the ears so funny."

Help the child hold up two fingers to be the "bunny."

"Here's the hole in the ground."

Make a circle with both hands for the hole.

"When a noise she hears,"

The bunny (the child) bends his or her ears down by bending the two upright fingers down toward the thumb.

"She picks up her ears,"

With a quick snapping motion, help the child stick his or her fingers straight up in the air.

"And jumps in the hole in the ground!"

Have the two fingers jump into the "hole" you made. Once the bunny is in the "hole," give the fingers a couple of loving squeezes.

Variations: When the little bunny jumps into the hole, you can give the child a kiss on the back of the hand. As the big bunny goes into the hole, you can give the child a hug.

Mr. Sun

Oh Mr. Sun, Sun
Mr. Golden Sun,
Won't you smile down
on my friend [say the child's name]?
Oh Mr. Sun, Sun
Mr. Golden Sun,
Won't you shine down
on my friend [say the child's name]?

Materials: Face paint or markers, preferably yellow for the sun and another color that matches the color of the child's eyes.

Preparation and Instructions: This is a song that is sung with the child while you draw a picture on the back of the child's hand. Sitting facing each other, begin the activity by holding the child's hand palm down. Have the markers or paint ready to use.

"Oh Mr. Sun, Sun"

Draw a round circle on the back of the child's hand to represent the sun.

"Mr. Golden Sun,"

Draw the rays of the sun radiating from the circle.

"Won't you smile down"

Draw a smiling face inside the circle. Make sure the sun's face is oriented toward the child, not toward you.

"On my friend [say the child's name]?"

Show the child the drawing.

"Oh Mr. Sun, Sun"

Trace around the circle to make it darker.

"Mr. Golden Sun,"

Trace over the sun's rays to make them darker.

"Won't you shine down"

Make the smiling face darker and more visible. You could add eye color to the face, perhaps matching the color of the child's eyes.

"On my friend [say the child's name]?"

Variations: Once the picture is drawn, you can place the child's hands back to back to transfer the picture from one hand to the other. The child will have two pictures instead of one!

On Your Face

On your face you have a nose.
And way down here you have ten
toes.
Two eyes that blink,
And a head to think.

You have a chin and very near,
You have two ears to help you hear.
Arms go high and arms go low
[Arms go low and arms go high]
A great big hug to say hello [to say
good-bye].

Preparation and Instructions: Sit in front of the child, either on the floor or in two chairs. Remember that your facial expressions need to be exaggerated and filled with delight.

"On your face you have a nose."

Touch your child's nose.

"And way down here you have ten toes."

Starting with your hands on the child's shoulders, slide down the child's arms and then touch or point to the child's toes.

"Two eyes that blink,"

Touch the child on the temples next to his or her eyes.

"And a head to think."

With both your hands, gently cradle the sides of the child's head.

"You have a chin and very near,"

Touch the child's chin.

"You have two ears to help you hear."

Touch both ear lobes and whisper something short into the child's ear. Some suggestions are, "I like you," "I am glad to see you," "I love you," "I'm glad you are my granddaughter."

I Love You
Rituals

108

"Arms go high and arms go low [Arms go low and arms go high]."

Grasp the child's wrists and hold the arms high over his or her head; then bring them back down (or vice versa if you are using the variant line).

"And a great big hug to say hello" [to say good-bye]."

Extend your arms and give the child a hug.

Variations: The last two lines can be changed as was indicated, depending on whether you are using the rhyme as a hello ritual or a good-bye ritual.

One, Two, Three, Four, Five

One, two, three, four, five,

I caught a fish alive.

Six, seven, eight, nine, ten,

I let him go again.

Why did you let him go?

Because he bit my finger so.

Which one did he bite?

The little one on the right.

Materials: Cake frosting or some kind of pudding goes well with this poem. Have a wet wipe or wet washcloth ready to clean up after the game is over.

Preparation and Instructions: Wash the child's hands.

Verse One: As you say "One, two, three, four, five, I caught a fish alive," dab cake frosting or pudding on the ends of the child's fingers. When you say "Six, seven, eight, nine, ten, I let him go again," do *not* put additional pudding or frosting on; just touch each finger on the child's other hand.

Verse Two: Say this verse while holding the child's hand with pudding on the fingers. When you come to the last line, "The little one on the right," have the child lick or suck the pudding off that finger. Repeat the last two lines of the poem. "Which one did he bite? The little one on the right." Have the child lick the pudding off the next finger. Continue repeating the last two lines until all the fingers are clean.

Cleaning Up: Wash the child's hands with the wet wipe or washcloth. This is probably the most important part of the game. It gives you time to nurture and care for the child. It allows you time to massage his or her hands and send the messages "I will care for you" and "I am here for you." Do not rush through this wonderful moment.

Round and Round the Garden

Round and round the garden
Goes the teddy bear.
One step, two step
Tickle under there.

Preparation and Instructions: Begin by holding your child's hand in your hand, palm up.

"Round and round the garden"

Draw circles on the child's hand with your index finger as you say, "Round and round the garden."

"Goes the teddy bear."

Continue drawing circles in cadence with the chant.

"One step, two step"

Walk your fingers up the child's arm (heading for the armpit).

"Tickle under there."

Give a gentle tickle under the child's arm.

There Was a Little Mouse

There was a little mouse
And she had a little house
And she lived
Up here.

Preparation and Instructions: This is the same type of game as "Round and Round the Garden."

"There was a little mouse"

Holding the child's palm, "walk" your fingers in his or her palm like a little mouse.

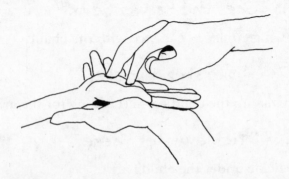

"And she had a little house"

Release the child's palm and encircle the child's hand with both your hands.

"And she lived"

Walk your two fingers up the child's forearm. With your tone of voice and facial expressions, build the child's anticipation of the next move.

"Up here."

Touch the child in a spot that would be a surprise. It could be the ear lobe, chin, top of the head, or nose.

Ten Little Candles

Ten little candles on a
chocolate cake,
Whew, whew,* now there are
only eight.
Eight little flickers on the
candlesticks,
Whew, Whew, now there are
only six.
Six little candles and not one more,
Whew, whew, now there are
only four.
Four little candles—red, white,
and blue,
Whew, whew, now there are
only two.
Two little candles standing in
the sun,
Whew, whew, now there is none.
The chocolate cake is in my sight.
I think I'll take a little bite.

_____

*Make two short air puffs, as if you are blowing out candles on a cake.

Preparation and Instructions: This delightful hand-and-finger interaction is great for a child's birthday. You can do it each day of the week before the great event.

"Ten little candles on a chocolate cake,"

With your hands slightly above the child's wrists, hold up both the child's hands so that the child's fingers are pointing up like birthday candles on a cake.

"Whew, whew, now there are only eight."

"Blow out" two of the fingers. Use enough focused blowing power so the child feels the air on his or her fingers. Simultaneously, assist the child in holding down those two fingers if needed.

"Eight little flickers on the candlesticks,"

"Whew, whew, now there are only six."

Continue blowing out the candles until all the fingers are down:

"Six little candles and not one more,"

"Whew, whew, now there are only four."

"Four little candles—red, white, and blue,"

"Whew, whew, now there are only two."

"Two little candles standing in the sun,"

"Whew, whew, now there is none."

"The chocolate cake is in my sight."

Look at the child's hand.

"I think I'll take a little bite."

Gently nibble on the child's hand, making exaggerated smacking noises with your lips.

The Hello Game

See my big finger [hand, foot,
thumb, elbow]
Crawling by you?
Here it comes—"Hello finger."
There it goes—"Good-bye finger."

See my big foot [hand, finger, elbow,
thumb]
Waving hello to you.
Here it comes—"Hello foot."
There it goes—"Good-bye foot."

"See my big finger"

Hold up your index finger so that the child can see it. You can use other body parts to play this game, for example, "See my big elbow."

"Crawling by you?"

Have your finger (hand, elbow, foot, or thumb) pass by the child's fingers (hand, elbow, foot, or thumb).

"Here it comes—'Hello finger.'"

Touch the child's finger with your finger as you say, "Hello, finger."

"There it goes—'Good-bye, finger.'"

Touch the child's finger and say, "Good-bye, finger." Move your finger out of the child's sight.

"See my big foot"

Hold up your foot so that the child can see it. Again, you can use any body part you wish. It is more fun if the body part used in the first verse is different from the body part used in the second verse.

"Waving hello to you?"

Wiggle your foot to say hello to the child.

"Here it comes—'Hello, foot.'"

Have your foot touch the child's foot.

"There it goes—'Good-bye, foot.'"

Touch the child's foot again and withdraw your foot, pretending to leave.

This Little Finger

This little finger went to school in a
car.
This little finger rode the bus.
This tall finger rode her [his] bicycle.
And this one chose to walk.
This thumb lived so-o-o far away.
It had to go up the hill and down.
Up the hill and down,
Up the hill and down,
Up the hill and around,
To get all the way inside the school.

Preparation and Instructions: This is a wonderful ritual to use with children when they begin preschool or kindergarten.

"This little finger came to school in a car."

Massage the child's little finger as you say this line. End the massage at the tip of the finger by giving it a loving squeeze as you say, "car."

"This other finger rode the bus."

Repeat the activity with the ring finger, giving a little squeeze on the word "bus."

"This tall finger rode her [his] bicycle."

Massage the middle finger and end with a squeeze as before.

"And this one chose to walk."

Repeat the process with the index finger.

"This thumb lived so-o-o far away"

As you say this line, hold the thumb firmly and wriggle it.

"It had to go up the hill and down."

Starting on the outside of the thumb, trace up to the top of the thumb. Then, slide down into the valley between the thumb and the child's index finger. Do this up-and-down movement to coincide with the corresponding words of the rhyme.

"Up the hill and down,"

Continue by going up the side of the index finger, over the top, and down into the valley between the index finger and the middle finger.

"Up the hill and down,"

Continue tracing the child's fingers.

"Up the hill and around,"

When you finish this tracing, you are between the ring finger and the little finger. As you say, "around," quickly trace up and down the little finger, then across the palm, back to the child's thumb.

"To get all the way inside the school."

Tuck the child's thumb into the palm of his or her hand. Wrap each of the child's fingers down over the thumb one at a time until all fingers make a fist with the thumb tucked inside (putting the thumb inside the school). End the interaction by encircling the child's fist with your hands in a loving, gentle squeeze.

This Little Finger Goes Night-Night

This little finger on the end
goes cluck, cluck like a baby hen.
The next little finger on the hand
goes [make a noise] like a big
brass band.
This tall finger goes tick tock,
just like Mommy's alarm clock.
This little finger points to you
and says, "I love you, yes I do."
The last little thumb goes
night-night.
And says, "Kiss me so I will
sleep tight."

Preparation and Instructions: Holding your child's hand, say the rhyme while you touch and massage the designated finger and make the appropriate noises. At the last line, give your child a kiss and tuck him or her in bed.

Today Is _____'s Birthday

Today is [say the child's name]
_____'s birthday.
Let's make her [him] a cake.
Mix and stir,
Stir and mix,
Then into the oven to bake.
Here is the cake so nice and round,
Frosted with pink and white,
We put five [or any other number]
candles on the top.
And blow out the birthday light.

Preparation and Instructions: This is a delightful way to help celebrate your child's birthday. Wake your child up with this ritual on the morning of his or her birthday.

"Today is [the child's name]'s birthday."

Looking the child in the eyes, say the first line with great love and joy.

"Let's make her [him] a cake."

Say this line with excitement. Rub your hands down the sides of the child's body.

"Mix and stir,"

Pretend to be mixing and stirring the child by massaging the child's arms.

"Stir and mix,"

Continue the massaging process with some gentle wiggling and jiggling of the child's entire body.

"Then into the oven to bake."

Pick the child up and lay him or her in your lap. Your lap is the pretend oven. It is fun to make a humming sound as if the child is cooking. For larger children, wrap your arms around their bodies.

"Here is the cake so nice and round,"

Take the child out of the oven by removing the child from your lap or unwrapping your arms.

"Frosted with pink and white."

Slide your hands down the child's arms, pretending to put on the cake frosting.

"We put five [or any other number] candles on the top,"

Help the child hold up as many fingers as the child is old.

"And blow out the birthday light."

Have the child blow on his or her own fingers. As the child blows, you can tuck the fingers away and snuggle the child in your arms. You can sing the traditional Happy Birthday song to the child while you rock the child in your arms.

Two Blackbirds

Two little blackbirds
Sitting on a hill.
One named Jack and
The other named Jill.

Fly away, Jack.
Fly away, Jill.
Come back, Jack.
Come back, Jill.

Two little blackbirds
Watching a show.
One named Fast and
The other named S-L-O-W.
Fly away, Fast.
F-l-y A-w-a-y, S-l-o-w.
Come back, Fast.
C-o-m-e b-a-c-k, S-l-o-w.

Two little blackbirds
Looking at the sky
One named Low and
The other named High.

Fly away, Low.
Fly away, High.
Come back, Low.
Come back, High.

Preparation and Instructions: Have the child sit on your lap with his or her back to your stomach, so you can reach around the child with your arms and manipulate the child's hands. Hold the child's hands in your hands as if you were going to control a puppet. Have the child make two fists and point his or her thumbs up in the air. Start each verse with both the child's hands behind the child's back.

"Two little blackbirds, sitting on a hill. One named Jack and"

Bring out one of the child's fists with the thumb pointing up.

"The other named Jill."

Bring out the other fist.

"Fly away, Jack."

Fly that hand back behind the child by moving the child's hand from the front of his or her body to the back.

"Fly away, Jill."

Fly that hand behind the child's back.

"Come back, Jack. Come back, Jill."

When the birds are called back, fly them to their position in front of the child.

The Other Verses: The rhyme proceeds in the same format for all verses. The only variation is the way the birds fly. For the bird named Fast, move the child's hand rapidly and speak rapidly. For the bird named Slow, move and speak slowly. When the bird's name is Low, speak in a low tone; when the bird's name is High, use a high tone.

Variations: You and the child can make up endless variations on the names of the birds. Have fun!

Warm Hands

Warm hands, warm.
Do you know how
To toast those little fingers?
I'll blow in your hands now!

Warm hands, warm.
Do you know how
To toast those little fingers?
I'll rub your hands now!

Preparation and Instructions: This is a wonderful interaction for winter days or any time you feel the child needs a "warming up."

"Warm hands, warm."

Take the child's hands in yours and rub them rapidly to warm them up.

"Do you know how"

Continue to move your hands over the child's hands.

"To toast those little fingers?"

Cup your hands over the child's hands. Make sure you are at eye level with the child.

"I'll blow in your hands now!"

Cup the child's hands in your hands, bring them to your mouth, and blow gently into the cavity created, warming the child's hands with your breath.

Verse Two: This verse is done the same way as verse one, but instead of blowing, rub the child's hands with your hands.

You Have Ten Little Fingers

You have ten little fingers,
And they all belong to you.
They are so very wonderful,
Look what they can do.
We can shut them up tight.
We can open them up wide.
We can put them all together,
And we can see what's inside.
We can open them up
and trace all the lines.
We can put them together,
Matching yours and mine.

Preparation and Instructions: Sit with the child so that you are facing each other.

"You have ten little fingers, and they all belong to you."

Touch each of your child's ten fingers as you say these two lines.

> "They are so very wonderful, look what they can do."

Continue to touch the child's hands and admire them. Look at the child with a sense of pride. When you say, "look what they can do," clap your child's hands together.

> "We can shut them up tight."

Take the child's hands and put them together into a tight ball.

> "We can open them up wide."

Open the child's hands and extend the child's fingers out wide.

> "We can put them all together, and we can see what's inside."

Tuck the child's hands together within yours and then open your hands slightly to peek inside.

> "We can open them up and trace all the lines."

Open the child's hands and use your finger to trace the lines in the child's palms.

"We can put them together, matching yours and mine."

Hold your hands palm to palm with the hands of the child. Clap your hands against the child's as you end the rhyme.

Your Fingers Are So Sleepy

Your fingers are so sleepy
It is time they went to bed.
First you, baby finger,
Tuck in your little head.
Ring finger, now it's your turn.
Then comes the tall one, this is
just great!
Pointer finger, hurry, because it's
getting late!
Is everyone here and nestled in?
No, there is one to come.
Move over, everyone, here comes
the thumb!

Preparation and Instructions: This is a wonderful interaction for nap time or bedtime. Keep your voice calm and soothing.

"Your fingers are so sleepy"

Yawn and speak slowly and softly. Hold the child's hand in one of your hands, palm facing upward, and gently stroke the child's hand.

"It is time they went to bed."

With your other hand, cover the child's hand as if to cover it up in bed.

"First you, baby finger,"

Remove your hand and begin to put the fingers to bed. Start with the pinky finger. Give this finger a gentle massage.

"Tuck in your little head."

Tuck the finger into the child's palm and hold it there with your supporting hand.

"Ring finger, now it's your turn."

Tuck down the next finger with the same loving care.

"Then comes the tall one, this is just great!"

Continue as before.

"Pointer finger, hurry, because it's getting late!"

Increase your speed of speech when saying this line, remembering to keep your tone soft.

"Is everyone here and nestled in?"

Massage the tops of the fingers and the child's knuckles.

"No, there is one to come."

With a surprised and concerned face, discover the thumb.

"Move over, everyone, here comes the thumb!"

Open all the fingers and tuck your child's thumb into his or her palm. Tuck the child's other fingers down over the thumb and encompass the child's hand with both of yours, like a cozy blanket.

Interactive
Finger
Plays

135

You've Been Gone

You've been gone and
You've been missed.
Here's an angel
For a hello kiss.

Preparation and Instructions: This is a great "welcome-back" ritual. Using a stuffed angel or animal for the kiss adds a delightful dimension; however, you can pretend to be the angel and give the kiss yourself.

"You've been gone and"

Hold the angel figurine or stuffed animal so that the child can see it as you say the first three lines of the poem. If you have no object, extend your arm and show the child your closed fist, with your thumb facing the child. Wiggle your thumb so that your fist looks like a mouth talking.

"You've been missed."

Continue to move the object or your hand playfully, closer to the child.

"Here's an angel"

Build the excitement with your facial expressions of delight and with the movement of the object.

"For a hello kiss."

Kiss the child with the object or with your hand. Finish the interaction with a big hug and a kiss.

Chapter
6

Silly Interactions

Angels can fly because they take
themselves lightly.

—Anonymous

Family Handshakes

Preparation and Instructions: To begin the game, greet the child with a big smile, "Good morning," and a handshake.

The Game: As you hold the child's hand, tell the child, "We are going to play a handshake game. After I shake your hand, I am going to add another movement to the handshake." You may give the handshake and then raise your thumb (have the child raise his or her thumb also) and touch thumbs together. Repeat the two-part handshake. Then add another movement to your handshake, perhaps sliding the hands apart. Repeat the handshake: Shake hands, touch thumbs, and slide apart. By now the child will have an idea of the game. Ask the child to add the next movement to the handshake. It may be a high five. Repeat the handshake: Shake hands, touch thumbs, slide apart, and do a high five.

Involve the whole family in creating a handshake. Each family member can add a movement. The handshake could then become a special family ritual for saying hello or good-bye.

Variations: Instead of doing handshakes, play the game pinky hugs. The game begins with the adult interlocking his or her pinky finger with the pinky finger of the child and announcing, "This is a pinky hug." Add different "hugs" to the pinky hug as you did in the handshake game. You can use elbow hugs, thumb hugs, and knee hugs. After you add each element, remember to repeat the entire series, always beginning with the pinky hug.

My Hand Is Stuck

Preparation and Instructions: This game begins by placing your hand on the child and saying, "My hand is stuck." It is a wonderful game to play if a child is hesitant to hold your hand or to stay close to you in public.

The Game: Pretend your hand is stuck on the child and that you cannot remove it no matter how hard you try. Next, look for the magic button that will free your hand. You may say and do the following:

"I wonder if the magic button is here?" Squeeze the child's thumb. "No, it is not there." Continue to struggle with your hand stuck on the child. "Maybe it is here." Push on the child's knee. "Nope! Now where can that button be?" Look all around the child. "I see it. I know where it is!" Push on the child's head with one finger while simultaneously freeing your other hand.

Greetings

Preparation and Instructions: The goal of this game is to be delightful and silly.

The Game: When the child arrives home from school, begin by shaking the child's hand and saying, "It is wonderful to see you." Then begin to get silly by shaking other body parts. Give a handshake to the child's foot, commenting, "It is wonderful to meet you, Mr. [or Ms.] foot." Shake the child's elbow, knee, pinky finger, earlobe, hair, thumbs, and nose. Any body part will do.

What Did You Bring Home from School Today?

Preparation and Instructions: When you greet the child after school, play this game.

The Game: Say to the child, "What did you bring home from school today?" Then begin taking inventory of all the things (body parts) the child brought home. You may say, "Oh, I see you brought your thumb, your shoulders, your two earlobes, . . ." As you name the body parts, touch each one.

It is important that you not mention any articles of clothing or other objects. The focus is on seeing and touching the child. Focusing on material items sends the message that what we own or possess is more important than who we are.

My Face Has a Gift for You

Preparation and Instructions: This game is similar to the traditional game called "pick a hand." In this old favorite, one person puts both hands behind his or her back with a secret object in one hand. Both hands are then brought from behind to be displayed to the person in front. The person must pick a hand to try to locate the object. If the person picks the hand containing the object, he or she gets to keep the surprise.

In this version of the game, you put your hands behind your back, but you are not holding an object. Simply put your hands behind your back and then bring them in front of you.

The Game: Ask the child, "Pick a hand, any hand." When the child selects a hand, briefly make a funny face with a noise. You may laugh out loud, giggle, growl, frown, sigh, and so forth.

Then put your hands behind your back again. Bring your hands forward and have the child select again. Make another face and continue the game. Keep the pace of this game fairly rapid.

Variations: As the child becomes familiar with the game, allow the child to be the leader. As the child makes faces, you attempt to copy the faces he or she makes.

Silly Me

Preparation and Instructions: These are delightful interactions with a child that alter the normal sequence of events or offer the element of surprise. The following is but a brief list of possibilities. The type of silly interaction you create is limited only by your imagination. Be playful; see how many different silly interaction games you can create.

The Game: Start with the following ideas and make up more.

1. Put the child's shoes on the wrong feet.
2. Put the child's shoe (or sock) on the child's hand; then try to put it on the child's elbow.
3. Push the child's nose (belly button, or another body part) and make a silly noise.
4. Comb the child's knee as if this were the natural and correct way to comb hair.
5. Blow raspberries on the child's hand, stomach, or other places. Name the noises by saying, "There is an elephant in your hand. See! Right there!" Then blow another raspberry. Blow three "elephant calls" and ask the child, "How many elephants did you hear?" Sometimes the raspberries sound more like ducks quacking. Use your imagination!

Jelly Bean Toes

Preparation and Instructions: This is a wonderful game to play while taking off children's shoes and socks. Sit with the child comfortably in front of you or in a chair.

The Game: Grasp one of the child's feet and begin to feel around inside the shoe. As you come to the toes, say, "I think there are jelly beans in here. I love jelly beans. Yum, Yum!" Proceed to take off the child's shoes while you continue to talk about jelly beans and how you can't wait to see them, taste them, and so on.

After you get the shoes off, continue the same process with the socks. You may say, "Now I know they are jelly beans. But wait, they are moving. Maybe they are jumping beans instead of jelly beans." Be sure your facial expressions are exaggerated. Pull off the socks and say with surprise and delight, "Well, they are toes! Wonderful, beautiful, perfect toes!" Pretend to nibble the "jelly beans." Many children have sand or dirt in their shoes. You may use this time to brush and clean the feet.

Yes and No Game

Preparation and Instructions: This is a wonderful game to play with a child who is a bit grumpy. Tell the child, "When I say, yes, you are to say, no. You will copy how I speak exactly. If I say yes very loudly, you will say no very loudly."

The Game: Begin by saying yes in your normal voice. Wait for the child to say, no in his or her normal voice. If the child appears not to understand the game, model both the yes and no for the child. Next, say yes in a high, squeaky voice; the child should respond no in a high, squeaky voice. Change your voice, tone, and pitch as you continue the game. Make sure to exaggerate your facial expressions and sounds. You could also shake your head yes and the child, in response, would nod his or her head no. You can be just as silly as you want to be. You can say yes while you laugh, sneeze, hiccup, or cry.

You Have a Present

Preparation and Instructions: This game can be played at Christmas, during Hanukkah, as part of a birthday celebration, or when you return from a trip and the child asks, "Did you bring me anything?"

The Game: Take some newspaper or scrap paper and wrap the paper around the child's hand. Use this time to touch the child affectionately. The goal is not to wrap the hand, but to connect with and touch the child. After the hand is wrapped, pretend to put a ribbon or bow on the top. Announce, "What a wonderful present; it looks beautiful. I wonder what is in it?" Begin to unwrap the hand slowly, expressing all your feelings and thoughts aloud. You may say, "I am so excited. This is the best present ever. I just can't wait to see it. I know it will be just perfect." As you get the hand partly unwrapped, reach under the paper to feel what may be inside. Comment on what you find. You may say, "Oh, what could this be? I think I found a finger. It is a wonderful finger, a perfect length, and a perfect color. Let me see. It is absolutely breathtaking in beauty. I wonder if there are more." Once you open your entire "gift," scoop the child up in your arms, expressing "I love you" in as many ways as you can think of. If you brought a "real" gift, a delightful time to give it to your child would be after this game.

Mama's Smart Girl [Boy]

Preparation and Instructions: This is a wonderful activity to help children go to school. It is especially useful at the beginning of the year when the transition from home to school is so difficult. The song is sung to the tune of "Mama's Little Baby Loves Shortening Bread."

The Game: Kneel down or pick up your child in your arms so that you are eye to eye. Sing the following song to your child:

> Mama's smart girl [boy] is precious, precious.
> Mama's smart girl [boy] is loved so much.
> Mama's smart girl [boy] will go to school.
> Mama's smart girl [boy] will meet the bus.
> Put on your socks. Put on your shoes.
> Going to school is wonderful news.

Chapter
7

Soothing and Relaxing
Games

Success is the ability to fulfill your
desires with effortless ease.

—Deepak Chopra

Goodnight Elbow

Preparation and Instructions: Add this delightful game to your child's bedtime routine.

The Game: Tell your child, "I am going to say goodnight to your ears, your hair, your forehead, your eyebrows, your shoulders, and your elbows." Continue down the child's body, saying goodnight to as many parts as you want to. Each time you say goodnight to a body part, touch that part. Each touch involves a gentle massage, helping your child relax for a good night of sleep. Take your time. Use the time to relax as well by emptying your mind of clutter and being totally present with your child.

Variation: In the morning, play "wake up elbow." Tell your child, "I am going to wake up your hair, your ears, your chin, your thumb, and so on. Touch each part that you "wake up."

Guess What I Am Writing [Drawing]?

Preparation and Instructions: To start this game, have the child turn around so his or her back is available to you as "pretend paper."

The Game: Tell the child, "I am going to write [or draw, depending on the child's age and reading level] something on your back. See if you can guess what I am writing [drawing]." Make sure that what you write or draw is easy for the child to guess. The goal of the game is to touch the child and enjoy one another. It is not to test the child on spelling or to put the child in a position where he or she may not be successful. You may want to write letters or numbers. In this case, tell the child, "I am going to write a letter on your back. See if you can guess what letter it is." For younger children, you may want to draw a shape. End the game with a relaxing back rub.

I LIKE
BEING
WITH YOU

I LOVE
YOU

Variations: You can also play a game called "two on a pencil." For this game you need a sheet of paper and a crayon, marker, pencil, or pen. Put your hand over the child's hand to guide the child to write the note. You may write, "I am glad to see you" or any other statement that celebrates the relationship between you.

Hot Dog Game

Materials: A baby blanket or beach towel.

Preparation and Instructions: Lay the towel or blanket flat on the floor. Have the child lie down across one end of the towel or blanket. Ultimately, you will be rolling the child in the blanket like a hot dog, using the blanket as a pretend bun. Be sure that the child's head and feet are outside the blanket.

The Game: Begin the game by saying, "I am going to pretend this towel is a hot dog bun and you are a hot dog. Lie down here on the bun. Boy, am I hungry. I sure would love a hot dog. Well, look here, I see a hot dog right in front of me. I need to put on some ketchup." Pretend to squirt ketchup on the child and rub it all around (massage the child). "I need some mustard." Continue to pretend putting as many things on the hot dog as you like. You may want to ask the child, "What do you like on your hot dog?" Once the hot dog has everything you like on it, roll the child up in the towel. Once the child is rolled up, you can put the child in your lap or leave him or her on the floor. Pretend to gobble up the hot dog.

Variations: You can roll the child up in the blanket and then say, "Oh, I forget to put the pickles on." Unroll the child to put on pickles. Roll the child in the blanket again. This variation allows you to roll the child securely in the blanket and unroll the child until he or she becomes more comfortable being wrapped tightly. This game is soothing for children who have attention deficit challenges. You can change the game from a hot dog to a burrito.

Putting Lotion on the Hurts

Materials: You will need a bottle of hand lotion, preferably a bottle with a pump spout.

Preparation and Instructions: This is a wonderful game to play with children after they have experienced some pain—either physical, as after a fall off a bike, or emotional, as after the death of a pet. Search the child for boo-boos—old scars or new scratches. The size or intensity of the scar or sore is not relevant.

The Game: Begin the game by saying, "I am going to put some lotion on all your hurts. I see one right here. I will be very careful." Continue looking over the child's body for hurts. If the hurt is old, lotion can be put directly on the scar. If the hurt is new, be careful to encircle the wound with lotion. Put some lotion on one finger and apply it gently. It is important that you repeat the message, "I will take care of you. No more hurts for you," as you apply the lotion. Sometimes the child will help you find the sores. While you are putting lotion on one sore, the child is locating the next sore. If this happens, say, "There are so many hurts, and you want me to notice them all. I will find them. I will not forget. See this one here. I am putting lotion all around it." Sometimes a child will tell you stories of how he or she was hurt. It is important to listen to the child.

Variations: A variation of this game is played with Band-Aids. You begin the game with at least two. Ask the child, "Where do these go?" The child will direct you to the spot where the Band-Aid should be placed. If it is a sore, speak to it, saying, "I am glad I found you. This Band-Aid is for you."

Tell Me When I Am at the End

Materials: A bottle of hand lotion.

Preparation and Instructions: This is a wonderful game to play by itself or in conjunction with the previous activity: putting lotion on the hurts. It is also a delightful way to put sunscreen on a child.

The Game: Begin the game by putting lotion on your hands and then rubbing it on the child's hand and arm. Beginning close to the elbow or shoulder, encircle the child's arm and slowly pull your hands down the arm in a massaging fashion. Say to the child, "Tell me when I get to the end." Slowly move down the arm to the hand and down the fingers until you get to the end of the longest finger, occasionally saying, "Am I at the end yet?" You may have to cue the child several times by saying, "Am I at the end yet?" If the child misses the end, simply state, "There it is. I found the end."

Variations: Do the same activity on the child's legs. Start at the thigh and work your way all the way down to the child's big toe.

Rub and Dry Game

Materials: You will need a terrycloth towel and a spray bottle containing water.

Preparation and Instructions: Have the child sit on your lap. Tell the child you are going to play rub and dry. This is a wonderful game for teaching children how to play respectfully with squirt guns with their friends.

The Game: Always tell the child what you are going to do before you do it, so you build trust. Using a spray bottle, spray water on the child's hand and then dry the child's hand with the terrycloth towel. Use this time to massage the child's hand and fingers. You may say, "I am drying off [child's name]'s perfect hand. This perfect hand has five fingers, little hairs on it, five freckles, and two scars. Continue with the other hand. It is more predictable (and therefore more relaxing) to spray one hand at a time. Ask the child, "What gets sprayed next?" The child may show you an elbow or knee. Repeat the spraying-and-drying process.

Variations: Reverse roles and have the child ask you, "What would you like sprayed?" Have the child spray and dry your hands or arm. If the child sprays an area that is uncomfortable, tell him or her. Say, "I don't like to be sprayed in the face. Spray my knees."

Have the child move the body part that was sprayed and catch it with the towel. You could also have the child put his or her hand on a piece of colored construction paper. As you spray the child's hand, the paper will get wet. When the hand is removed from the paper, the dry area will be a hand print.

Move What I Touch

Materials: This game can be played without any materials or with many types of textured objects that you will use to touch the child. Such items as feathers, a terrycloth washcloth, a silk scarf, and even sandpaper are fun.

Preparation and Instructions: This is a wonderful game to play with individual children with developmental delays or who exhibit extremely distractable or impulsive behaviors. Many children who must cope with hyperactivity have trouble moving just one part of their bodies; when one part moves, the whole body moves. This game helps the children integrate and then differentiate body parts. Practicing in a gamelike situation with you will help them become more organized in school.

The Game: With the child lying on the floor in front of you, begin the game by telling the child, "I am going to touch a part of your body with my hand [finger]. I want you to move just that part of your body. The first body part I am going to touch is your index (or pointer) finger. See if you can move that finger and nothing else. Well, you did it. You just moved that one finger. You are good at this game. I am going to make it harder now. I am going to touch your whole hand. Well, look at that! You can do that, too. The rest of your body was perfectly still. You kept your legs still [rub your hands over the child's legs]. You kept your face still [rub your hands over the child's face]." Continue the game by touching other body parts.

Variations: Have the child play the game with his or her eyes closed. Touch the child with different textured objects. Remember, do not tickle. Tickling distracts the child from the purpose of the game.

Story Hand

Preparation and Instructions: Play this game when something wonderful has happened to your child or when you want to point out all the child's successes.

The Game: Tell the child, "It is story time." The child will probably think you are going to read a book, but instead, take her hand. Starting with the pinky finger, give this finger a nice massage and say, "This little finger wanted to learn how to ride a two-wheel bicycle." (The story you will be telling will be based on your child's life. I am using the success story of learning to ride a two-wheeler as an example.) Go to the next finger and give it a nice massage, saying, "This finger was a little scared she [or he] may fall off." Continue to the next finger, saying, "But this finger said, 'I can do it. I just know I can.'" At the index finger, continue with the story by saying, "So I decided to try and try again." Finally, come to the thumb and with excitement have the thumb say, "Did she [or he] do it? Did she [or he] do it?" Then tuck the thumb into the palm of the child's hand and say, "No problem. All the fingers knew she [or he] would do it all the time."

Variations: This is a wonderful game to play with children who are anxious about something. As you rub each finger, express the child's unspoken concerns. When you get to the thumb, you can find a way to end the story that reassures your child. This is a powerful game. Be creative in making up the stories, as well as in the times you decide to use this strategy to help your child express and cope with his or her feelings.

Chapter
8

Hide-and-Seek Games

You have come here to find what you
already have.

—Buddhist aphorism

Find the Stickers

Materials: Use commercially bought stickers. Children love stickers, which make wonderful, surprise gifts.

Preparation and Instructions: Before you see the child, take four or five of the stickers and hide them on your head. At the beginning, make sure the stickers can be easily found. You may want to put one sticker on each earlobe, like earrings, and one sticker on your forehead, under your hair if possible. Be creative!

The Game: Begin the game by saying to the child, "I have hidden four stickers on my face. See if you can find them." As the child begins to look for them, use the skill of tracking. (Tracking is simply saying out loud what the child is doing. It is similar to the radio announcer at a ball game. You may say, "You are looking over by my ears, Aha! You found one. Now you are taking it off very gently and handing it to me.") As the child hands you the stickers, put one sticker on each finger of one hand as a holding place. From this holding place you are ready to play the game again or to play a variation of the game.

Variations: Once the child has located all the stickers, you can begin to play the "sticker-swap game" by saying, "I am going to

take this sticker off my thumb and put it on my chin." You proceed to do so. Then tell the child, "Take the sticker off my chin
and put it on your nose." From this point, you begin a turn-
taking game in which you remove the sticker from the child's
face and place it on your face. The child then removes the
sticker from your face and puts it on his or her face. Each
movement of the sticker is noted out loud. You speak for yourself and for the child, unless the child catches on and begins to
speak for himself or herself. Your observations may sound like
this:

"I am going to take the sticker off your chin and put it on my
nose. Now you are taking it off my nose and putting it on your
[wait for the child's selection] ear."

Find the Yarn

Materials: You will need about five or six strands of yarn, vary-ing in length from 12 inches to 6 feet. It is best to have a differ-ent color for each strand.

Preparation and Instructions: Before you meet the child, hide the yarn on your body. You may want to put yarn up your sleeve and in your pockets or socks. Wherever you put a strand, leave a piece sticking out for the child to spot. This is a won-derful game to play as a ritual when you return from a busi-ness trip and a child asks, "What did you bring me?"

The Game: Begin the game by telling the child, "I have hid-den four strands of yarn on my body. Find them and pull them out." As the child spots the tiny ends, she or he will begin to pull. Some of the strands will be short, and some will seem to go on forever. Track what the child is doing, as you did in the game of find the stickers. You may say, "You are looking around my arms. You see the pink yarn. You are pulling and pulling and pulling."

Once the yarn is out, you can be creative in what to do with it. You can measure the length of the child's body parts. You can stuff the yarn into the child's hand and have him or her throw it on your signal: "Ready, set, throw the yarn. Now find another piece of yarn." If the child has trouble locating the yarn, you can give helpful hints like the following: "I will give you a hint; it is below my knees" or "My eyes will look at it. Watch my eyes. My eyes are giving you a clue." Sometimes the child will need assistance. The goal of this challenging game is always for the child to be successful.

Hello, Toes/Good-bye, Toes

Preparation and Instructions: This game is wonderful to play while dressing or undressing your child. Take off the child's shoes and socks.

The Game: Once the shoes and socks are off the child's feet, bring one of the child's feet close to your face or move your face close to the child's foot and say, "Hello, toes." At this point you could look at them, blow on them, count them, touch them, or nibble at them. Quickly say, "Good-bye, toes" and hide the toes from your sight. Then begin with a hide-and-seek dialogue: "Where did those toes go? I just had them in my hand. They were so lovely. Now I have lost them. Oh dear, what will I do? Maybe I put them here." (Search for the feet all over the child.) Continue the game by taking off the child's shirt. You then can move close to the child's hand and say, "Hello, hand." Play the game with the hands, knees, elbows, shoulders, or any other body part.

Can You Find It?

Materials: Cotton balls and a favorite finger food.

Preparation and Instructions: Hide-and-seek games are really an extension of peek-a-boo games. The following two games are just examples. You can build on them as new games emerge between you and the children you play with.

Hide the Cotton Ball: Have the child sit or lie down in front of you and then hide three or four cotton balls somewhere around his or her body. The child may put them under a sleeve, in a pocket, or in a sock. Tell the child to give the signal when they are all hidden. The signal may be "Ready!" Begin to search for the cotton balls. Begin by saying, "Where could that cotton ball be? Maybe it is behind your ears. No, I know, maybe in your mouth. OK, you are tricking me. Is it in those ears?" Continue looking, touching, and talking—the sillier the better. You may say, "I need a hint." Ask the child to move his or her eyes in the direction of the cotton ball's location, so you can follow where the child is looking.

Hide the Food: When you find the food, feed it to the child. It is important that you give the food to the children immediately after you find it. Food represents love; never tease children with food. You want the message to be, "I will take care of you. I see you. You are loved and lovable." Remember to keep count of how many pieces the child has hidden. Sometimes pieces of food disappear!

I'm Hiding

I'm hiding, I'm hiding,
No one will find me here.
I'll be as quiet as I can be
When anyone gets near.
And when they've looked all over,
Around and all about,
I'll jump out from my hiding place
And give a great big shout.
"It's me!"

Materials: Two small baby blankets or beach towels.

Preparation and Instructions: Sitting side by side, cover the child and yourself each with a blanket.

The Game: When you get to the part about giving a great big shout, both of you pop out from under the blankets and shout, "It's me!" After you model this game with your child, the child will soon be able to hide by himself or herself and jump out on cue.

Variations: Instead of shouting, "It's me," you or the child could vary the ending response. The child may shout, "Here I am." In response you would say, "There you are, and I am so glad. I thought you were gone. I missed you." The child may say, "Boo!" Your response may be, "You wanted to scare me. I

see your brown eyes and black hair. I am glad to see you."
Whatever the child shouts, you respond by sending the message, "I see you. I am glad you are you. I missed you while you were gone."

Hide-and-Seek
Games

179

Peek-a-Boo. I See You!

Materials: This game can be played without any materials or with towels, scarves, or any other objects that you or the child can hide behind.

Preparation and Instructions: This is a traditional game that most people have played. You may play the game by covering your face or the child's face.

The Game: Begin the game with one of you hiding behind one of the objects. Then proceed by saying, "Where is Ashley? Where could she be? She was just here. Is she in my shoe? Is she under the rug? Is she in my hand?" Look in silly places. Continue until you find the child. When you find her, say, "There you are!" Then describe what you see. You may say, "I see your blue eyes, your pinky finger, and your two knees." By describing the child to herself, you become a mirror for her. This mirroring strengthens your child's brain, literally wiring her for future self-control.

Peek-a-boo!

Where Are Those Hands?

Clap our hands, one-two-three.
Play a clapping game with me.
Whoops, your hands have
gone away.
I'll find your hands so we can play.

Preparation and Instructions: Sit with the child facing you. The game involves a clapping pattern. The simplest pattern is for the child to clap his hands together. To challenge your child, teach him to pat his thighs and then clap his hands. The most difficult pattern is for the child to pat his thighs, clap his hands, and then clap his hands together with yours. If the child is capable, you can use this pattern. Use the clapping pattern that creates the most success for you and your child.

"Clap our hands, one-two-three."

Say the words, "Clap our hands." Then, as you say, "one-two-three," clap your hands together and have your child clap his hands together three times.

"Play a clapping game with me."

As you say this line, play one of the clapping patterns just mentioned with the child. Ultimately, you want the child to pat his thighs twice (as you pat your thighs), clap his hands together twice (as you clap your hands), and clap his hands with yours three times.

"Whoops, your hands have gone away."

Have your child hide his hands. He may put them behind his back, under his legs, or in his shirt.

"I'll find your hands so we can play."

Locate the child's hands and hold them. Once the hands are found, start the rhyme again. Repeat the game as long as you are having fun.

Where Did It Go?

Preparation and Instructions: This is a familiar game to many adults. Many of us may have played this game with our parents or grandparents. I remember my grandfather coming up to me and saying, "I got your nose!" Then he would show me his thumb tucked between his fingers. I loved this game when I was a child.

The Game: Pretend to take the child's nose, finger, or other body part. Once you "take" a body part, it is important to put it back. You can use your imagination to help decide how to get the body part back on the child. Some suggestions of how to do so are as follows:

1. Kiss it back on.
2. Blow it back on.
3. Pretend to nail it back on.
4. Use a dab of lotion and pretend to glue it back on.

Variations: Sometimes the child will imitate this game and initiate the interaction by taking one of your body parts. The meaning of this is basically, "I like you enough to want to have a part of you." The child in effect is saying, "Do you like me enough to play my game? Will you come looking for me without your eyes? Can you breathe without your nose? Can you find me without your hands? Will you trust me to give them back to you?" Your response to the child is important. As the child begins this game, you may respond, "What happened to my eyes? I can't see Karen. Where did she go? Is this Karen? This feels like her fingers, feels like her toes." Or if the child takes your mouth, you may mumble, "I can hardly talk. Where is my mouth so that I can say, 'I love you?'"

Chapter
9

Cuddling and Snuggling
Games

The time to relax is when you don't have
time for it.

—Sidney J. Harris

Snuggle Time

Sometimes I yell.
Sometimes I hurry.
Sometimes I fuss.
And sometimes I worry.

All is not lost.
Everything is fine.
I love you so much.
Now it's snuggle time!

Preparation and Instructions: Each day, designate a "snuggle time." This is a five-minute time-out from the hustle of life.

The Game: To make a gentle transition from a busy time to a snuggle time, say the rhyme. This rhyme is the signal for both you and the child to locate each other and settle in together. Snuggle time is the time to hold each other, rock in a chair, or read a book.

Blanket Swing

Materials: This game requires two adults and a sturdy blanket large enough to hold the child.

Preparation and Instructions: Lay the blanket on the floor and position the child in the blanket. Each adult holds onto the two corners of the blanket.

The Game: On a signal given by one adult, the child is lifted up, cradled in the blanket. The adults swing the child gently in the blanket and sing a song. The child is then placed back on the floor on a signal. You may say, "Let's put her down on three. Ready? One, two, three." The signal trains the child to listen carefully. The message is, "If you listen carefully, you will then know what will happen to you." Verbally track the landing so the child knows exactly what is about to happen. You may say, "Let's put her bottom down first, then her feet, and carefully lay her head down." There are many lullaby tunes that can be sung as you swing the child gently from side to side. Such songs as "Rock-a-Bye Baby" or "Brahms Lullaby" are soothing. If you choose to sing "Rock-a-Bye Baby," I suggest that you change the ending. The traditional ending is as follows:

When the bough breaks,
the cradle will fall.
And down will come baby,
cradle and all.

For a more secure message to the child, the following ending is recommended:

When the bough breaks,
the cradle will fall.
And I will catch the cradle,
baby and all.

Cuddling and
Snuggling
Games

189

Row, Row, Row Your Boat

Row, row, row your boat
Gently down the stream.
Merrily, merrily, merrily, merrily
Life is but a dream.

Preparation and Instructions: Sit on the floor with your legs crossed. Have the child sit in your lap with his back to your front. Put your arms around the child, holding him snugly. The child is now sitting inside a wonderful, cozy "boat."

The Game: Rock side to side or back and forth as you sing the song. After you sing the song once, say to the child, "Oh, my gosh, a storm is coming. I have to hold you tight so you won't fall out of the boat." At this point, begin to roll around from side to side as if the boat were in stormy waters, holding the child closer and closer. Sing the song again in a loud, stormy voice. After you sing the song one time in stormy seas, say, "The storm is over, the sea is calm." Return to your gentle rocking side to side and back and forth, singing the song once again in a calm, soothing voice.

Variations: My grandfather used to play this game with me.* During the storm part, he would say, "Oh no, we have hit a rock. We are going down. I will save you." Then he would lift me up and put me on his shoulders to save me from drowning in the sea. From here he would carry me to the dinner table or to bed.

Cuddling and
Snuggling
Games

191

---

*Even though I had played this game as a child with my grandfather, I was formally taught this game in a workshop led by Dr. Viola Brody.

Snuggle Up

Preparation and Instructions: A "safe place" is an alternative to time out. A safe place is a place where children who are feeling rejected, alone, anxious, or angry can go to return themselves to a more peaceful inner state. Children cannot do so, however, unless they are first taught how to "calm down." Everyone gets upset; one important life skill is to be able to calm oneself down. To help your child learn to calm down, provide a safe place for your child. A beanbag chair is a wonderful safe place because it hugs you when you sit in it. To teach your child how to use the safe place, sit with the child in it, holding the child and a transition object, such as a teddy bear. While sitting in the beanbag chair, hold the child and sing the following to the tune of "Rock-a-Bye Baby":

> Snuggle up children
> In your safe place.
> You can go there,
> To have your own space.
> When you feel scared
> And want to feel loved,
> Just cuddle yourself
> And the bear with a hug.

When you get to the last two lines of the song, hold the child and the bear tightly, giving an extra little hug. Tell your child that when she is angry or upset, she can come to the safe place to calm down. To do so, hug the bear and take two long breaths. You must show the child how to calm down as you sit in the chair snuggling them. To teach the child what a safe place is and what it is for, this activity must be repeated over and over again. Eventually, the child will be able to go to the safe place alone and feel the same soothing feelings she or he felt with you.

Held in My Arms

Preparation and Instructions: This activity is both an inter-action and a song. Sing the song to the tune of "Rock-a-Bye Baby."

The Game: While holding your child in your arms, sing the following song:

> Rock-a-bye baby
> Held in my arms.
> Having you near me, I see your charms.
> When things seem scary, I'll hold you tight,
> And whisper, "I love you" all through the night.

Variations: Make up different verses. Substitute your child's name for the word "baby." Sometimes the song can be serious, and sometimes it can be silly. Have your child help you find rhyming words.

Chapter
10

Physically Active
Games

If play is to be genuine, it must be lighthearted
and pursued without purpose. That is why we
usually fail if we try to have fun.

—Larry Dossey

Blanket Volleyball

Materials: A towel or baby blanket and a balloon or a soft ball.

Preparation and Instructions: Hold two ends of the blanket and have the child hold the other two ends.

The Game: Place a ball or balloon in the middle of the blanket. On a signal given by you, you and the child toss the ball into the air and catch it in the blanket. Use visual signals, such as "When I blink my eyes, it means go." Use auditory signals, such as "1, 2, 3, go!" You may also say that the signal is a word, such as "alligator." Then you would say, "Always, apple, alligator." Auditory and word signals help the child learn to listen.

To structure this game:

1. Clearly state the goal of the game. "Our goal is to work together to toss the ball and catch it. We can count how many times we are able to do so."
2. Clearly give a signal: "The signal to begin the game will be 'ready, set, go.'"

3. To ensure that the child waits for the signal and is successful, do not put the ball on the blanket until just before the
signal to go.

Cotton Ball Blow

Materials: Cotton balls and a table to play on.

Preparation and Instructions: Sit across the table from the child, holding the child's arms with your arms to outline the playing field. Place a cotton ball in the middle of the field. On your signal, both of you will begin to blow. The object of the game is for the child to blow the cotton ball over to your chest and for you to blow the cotton ball over to the child's chest (or off the table, as the case may be). This is a great game to teach children how to observe the results of a game, instead of focusing only on winning or losing.

Important Points to Remember: This is not a competition. The child may attempt to turn it into one. To structure the game to reduce or prevent competition, you may want to do the following:

1. Begin the game by saying, "This game is called 'Cotton Ball Blow.' I will give a signal, and we will both blow the cotton ball to see where it goes. You will try to blow it over to me, and I will try to blow it over to you."

2. Tell the child the signal. "The signal will be ready, set, go. When I say 'go,' you and I will begin to blow."
3. Do not remove your hand from the cotton ball until you say go, so the child always begins on your signal and is successful.
4. If the child comments, "I won, I won," you can simply say, "You blew the cotton ball over to my side."
5. Verbally track the results of each blowing encounter. "You blew the cotton ball, and it hit our arms and flipped off the table."

The Big Crash

Preparation and Instructions: Pick the child up and swing him or her in the air.

The Game: Hold the child and swing him or her around. You can say, "Look at the airplane, soaring through the sky. Oh, no! Bumpy weather! It looks like a storm. We are crashing!" As you say, "We are crashing," fall gently to the floor with the child in your arms. Then continue the story by saying, "What a crash! I need to check you out to make sure that nothing was hurt." Remember to touch the parts of the body that you look at. You may say, "This arm looks good, and these eyebrows are OK. Oh look, your freckle survived! You've got all five fingers on this hand," and so on. After all the parts are checked, take off again. Continue running into poor weather or running out of gas to keep playing the game.

The Cat and the Bunny

Creeping, creeping, creeping,
Comes the little cat.
But the bunny with the long ears,
Hops like that.

Preparation and Instructions: Stand behind the child and prepare to move his or her body as you say the rhyme.

"Creeping, creeping, creeping,"

From behind the child, place your arms under the child's arms (so the child's armpits are resting on your arms) and hold onto the child's wrists. Move the child's arms in a creeping movement.

"Comes the little cat."

Continue to move the child's arms in a creeping motion. You may want to add a meow at the end of the line.

"But the bunny with the long ears,"

Raise the child's hands to either side of his or her head like big bunny ears.

"Hops like that."

Pick the child up grabbing under the armpits and take the child for a three-hop ride, one hop for each word in this line.

Variations: Change the movement at the end of the rhyme. You could say, "swings like that" as you swirl the child around through the air. Try, "leaps like that," "runs like that," "skips like that," or whatever you come up with at the moment.

Physically
Active
Games

203

Walk and Stop

Preparation and Instructions: Pick the child up in your arms.

The Game: Sing or chant the following words with any tune that works for you: "You walk and you walk and you walk and . . . STOP!" As you sing this song, take steps with the child in your arms. When you say, "STOP," bring your body to a quick halt. Repeat the song as you move around the room carrying the child.

Variations: Change the movements as you carry the child. Change from walking to jumping. You jump and you jump and you jump and . . . STOP! Try swaying, swinging, marching, skipping, hopping, wiggling, and leaping. Let your imagination go!

Bibliography

Bailey, B. A. (2000). *Easy to Love, Difficult to Discipline*. New York: HarperCollins.

Brody, V. A. (1993). *The Dialogue of Touch: Development Play Therapy*. Treasure Island, Fla.: Developmental Play Training Associates.

Brody, V., Stephenson, S., & Fenderson, C. (1976). *Sourcebook for Developmental Play*. Treasure Island, Fla.: Developmental Play Training Associates.

Davis, P. (1991). *The Power of Touch*. Carson, Calif.: Hay House.

Gibran, K. (1976). *The Prophet*. New York: Alfred A. Knopf.

Greenspan, S., & Greenspan, N. (1989). *First Feelings: Milestones in the Emotional Development of Your Baby and Child*. New York: Penguin Books.

Imber-Black, E., & Roberts, J. (1992). *Rituals for Our Times: Celebrating, Healing, and Changing Our Lives and Our Relationships*. New York: HarperCollins.

Jensen, E. (1997). *Completing the Puzzle: The Brain Compatible Approach to Learning*. Del Mar, Calif.: The Brain Store.

Jernburg, A. (1979). *Theraplay*. San Francisco: Jossey-Bass.

Karen, R. (1998). *Becoming Attached: First Relationships and How They Shape Our Capacity to Love*. New York: Oxford University Press.

Kohn, A. (1993). *Punished by Rewards: The Trouble with Gold Stars, Incentive Plans, A's, Praise and Other Bribes*. Boston: Houghton Mifflin.

Kotulak, R. (1997). *Inside the Brain: Revolutionary Discoveries of How the Mind Works*. Kansas City, Kans.: Andrews McMeel.

LeDoux, J. (1996). *The Emotional Brain: The Mysterious Underpinngs of Emotional Life*. New York: Simon & Schuster.

Montagu, A. (1986). *Touching: The Human Significance of the Skin* (3rd ed.). New York: Harper & Row.

Montagu, A. (1971). *Touching*. New York: Harper & Row.

Schore, A. N. (1994). *Affect Regulation and the Origin of the Self: The Neurobiology of Emotional Development*. Mahwah, N.J.: Lawrence Erlbaum Associates.

Solomon, J., & George C. (1999). *Attachment Disorganization*. New York: Guilford Press.

Index

Acceptance, 3, 40, 48
Adrenaline, 45–46
Arousal system, 19
Attachment, 14–15, 20
Attention seeking, 34, 35, 43–44
Attention span, 7, 9
Authority, 29–31

"Ba Ba, Black Sheep," 87–88
Baby games, 43–44
Bedtime, 42, 54
"Big Crash, The," 201
Birthdays, 52, 56, 114–16, 123–24
"Blanket Swing," 188–89
"Blanket Volleyball," 197–98
Bond, parent-child, 8–9, 14–17, 20
Brain, 4, 6, 7–9, 11, 27
    development of, 17–18, 31–32
    dopamine system and, 8–9
    stress and, 45–46
    wiring for self-control, 31–33
Brody, Viola, 41

"Can You Find It?," 176–77
"Cat and the Bunny, The," 202–3
Celebrations, rituals for, 56
Challenges, children who have
    experienced, 49–51, 55–56
Challenging children, 18–19
Change, 53–55
Chapin, Henry, 10
"Chase me" games, 42–43
Clutter, mental, 39
Communication, 8–9, 10
Conflicts, 9–10, 25, 29, 34
Connection, 5, 7, 13
Control, 18, 41, 42–43, 45, 49
    fostering feelings of, 19–20
    other- vs. self-, 27, 29–31
Cooperation, 7, 9, 17, 27, 29, 30
Cortisol, 46

"Cotton Ball Blow," 199–200
Cuddling games, 185–94

"Dancing Hands," 93–95
Delayed gratification, 27
Diamond, Miriam, 31
Discipline, 23–35
    parental power and, 29–31
    two common mistakes in, 28–29
Dopamine, 8–9
Dressing, rituals for, 54

Emotional disconnection, 34–35
Expectations, 40
Eye contact, 8–10, 15, 46

Facial expressions, 20
"Family Handshakes," 141–42
Fear, 13
Feedback, need for, 31–32
"Find the Stickers," 171–72
"Find the Yarn," 173–74
Finger plays, interactive, 91–137
"Five Little Babies," 96–98
Friendships, 17, 20

"Georgie Porgie," 69–70
Good-byes, rituals for, 54–55
"Goodnight Elbow," 155
"Greetings," 144
Growing milestones, rituals for,
    54
"Growing Up," 44, 99–100
Grumpy children, 56
"Guess What I Am Writing [Draw-
    ing]," 156–57
Guilt, 29, 30

Handshakes, family, 141–42
Healing, 55–56
"Held in My Arms," 194

"Hello, Toes/Good-bye, Toes," 175
"Hello Game, The," 117–18
Hellos, rituals for, 54–55
"Here's the Beehive," 101–2
"Here's the Bunny," 103–4
Hide-and-seek games, 41–42,
    49–50, 55, 169–84
Hippocampus, 46
"Hot Cross Buns," 76–78
"Hot Dog," 158–59
"Humpty Dumpty," 67–68

I Love You Rituals:
    goals of, 7–18, 39
    steps to playing, 40–41
    tips for, 39–40
"I'm asleep" game, 44
Imber-Black, Evan, 52–53
"I'm Hiding," 178–79
Infant carriers, 11

"Jack Be Noodle," 85–86
"Jelly Bean Toes," 149
Jensen, Eric, 27
Judging, noticing vs., 32–33

Language, 20
    of young children, 41–45
Learning potential, 11
Limits, 34, 48
"Little Bo Peep," 74–75
"Little Miss Muffet," 65–66
Losses, 14, 47, 55
Love, 39
    unconditional, 3, 4, 5, 26–28

"Mama's Smart Girl [Boy]," 152
"Margie Pargie," 71
"Mary, Mary, Extraordinary,"
    79–80
"Mary Had a Little Lamb," 72–73

Misbehavior, 34, 55
"Mr. Sun," 105–6
Motivation, 26–28, 45, 46
"Move What I Touch," 165–66
"My Face Has a Gift for You,"
    146–47
"My Hand Is Stuck," 143

Nerve growth factor, 11
Neurotransmitters, 8
Noticing, 31–33
Nursery rhymes, positive, 57–90

"One, Two, Three, Four, Five,"
    109–10
"On Your Face," 107–8

Parenting, mechanics vs. emo-
    tional aspects of, 15–17
"Peek-a-Boo. I See You!," 180
Peek-a-boo games, 19, 41–42,
    49–50
Permissive parenting, 29, 30
"Peter, Peter, Pumpkin Eater," 62
Physically active games, 195–204
Playfulness, 4, 49
Powerlessness, feelings of, 34
Punishment, 26
"Putting Lotion on the Hurts,"
    160–61

Relationships, 53
    roles vs., 5–6
Relaxing games, 153–68
Resistance, 7, 18–19, 28–29, 34,
    48, 49
Responsiveness, 20
Rewards, 26–28
Rituals, 12–13, 51–52
    purposes of, 52–53
    routines vs., 6–7

Rituals (*cont.*)
   suggested times for, 52
   see also I Love You Rituals
Roberts, Janine, 52–53
Roles, relationships vs., 5–6
"Round and Round the Garden,"
   111
Routines, rituals vs., 6–7
"Row, Row, Row Your Boat,"
   190–91
"Rub and Dry," 163–64

Safe place, 192
School, rituals for going to or
   returning from, 54
Self-awareness, 44–45
Self-esteem, 6, 14, 28, 32
Sexual abuse, 11
Sharing, 20
Silly interactions, 139–52
"Silly Me," 148
Skin, 11
"Snuggle Time," 187
"Snuggle Up," 192–93
Snuggling games, 185–94
Social interactions, 8, 19, 20
Soothing games, 153–68
"Stealing" body parts, 44
"Story Hand," 167–68
Stress, 10, 45–47
  severe, chronic, 47–49

"Tell Me When I Am at the End,"
   162
Temperament, 17
"Ten Little Candles," 114–16
"There Was a Little Mouse,"
   112–13
"This Little Finger," 119–21
"This Little Finger Goes Night-
   Night," 122
"Three Nice Mice," 89–90
Tickling, 50

"Today Is _____'s Birthday,"
   123–24
Toddlers, 28, 43, 56
"To Market, to Market," 81–82
Touch, 8, 9–12, 50
   fear of, 10–11
   inadequate, effects of, 10
   initiated by child, 44
   as metaphor, 11
Transitions:
   during day, 51–52
   in life, 53–55
Tuning out, 9
Turn taking, 20
"Twinkle, Twinkle, Little Star,"
   63–64
"Two Blackbirds," 125–27

Uncertainty, 19

Volleyball, blanket, 197–98

Waking, rituals for, 51–52, 54
"Walk and Stop," 204
"Warm Hands," 128–29
"Wee Willie [Wendy] Winkie,"
   83–84
"What Did You Bring Home from
   School Today?," 145
"Where Are Those Hands?,"
   181–82
"Where Did It Go?," 183–84
Whining, 43–44, 46
"Wonderful Woman Who Lived in
   a Shoe, A," 59–61

"Yes and No Game," 150
"You Have a Present," 151
"You Have Ten Little Fingers,"
   130–32
"Your Fingers Are So Sleepy,"
   133–35
"You've Been Gone," 136–37

Other Works by Dr. Becky Bailey

CDs and Cassettes
Songs for I Love You Rituals: Twenty-nine of the I Love You Rituals have been set to delightful music by Mar Harmann. By combining touch and music in an atmosphere of love, optimal brain development is supported.

Videotapes
Touch a Heart, Teach a Mind: The Brain-Smart Way to Build Bonds: See the I Love You Rituals in action! Watch parents, teachers, and Dr. Bailey interact with children, demonstrating how these rituals can be done in schools and homes.

Books
Easy to Love, Difficult to Discipline: The groundbreaking book sharing the parenting approach called Loving Guidance. Parents learn the skills necessary to turn conflict into cooperation. By viewing conflict as a teaching opportunity rather than as disrespect, parents can teach children the social skills needed for a lifetime of success.

Conscious Discipline: Brain Smart Classroom Management for Elementary Schools: The program uses everyday conflicts to teach social skills, character development, and conflict-resolution skills.

Shubert's BIG Voice: A children's book that teaches children how to deal with bullies.

Audiotapes
Dr. Bailey's tapes have won the prestigious Parents' Choice Award and the Parent's Guide Media Award.

> 10 Principles of Positive Discipline
> Preventing Power Struggles
> Transforming Aggression into Healthy Self-Esteem
> Brain Smart
> Conflict Resolution

Keynotes and Lectures
Becky Bailey is available for workshops and keynote addresses. Her dynamic presentations on Loving Guidance for parents and Conscious Discipline for schools have brought her worldwide acclaim. To schedule her in your area, call 1-800-842-2846, or visit her on the Web at: www.beckybailey.com.

BOOKS BY BECKY A. BAILEY, Ph.D.

EASY TO LOVE, DIFFICULT TO DISCIPLINE
The 7 Basic Skills for Turning Conflict into Cooperation

ISBN 0-06-000775-3 (paperback)

Dr. Becky Bailey's unusual and powerful approach to parenting has made thousands of families happier and healthier. Focusing on self-control and confidence-building for both parent and child, Dr. Bailey teaches a series of linked skills to help families move from turmoil to tranquillity. This seven-week program gets families off to a good start, offering plenty of real-life anecdotes that illustrate Dr. Bailey's methods at work.

I LOVE YOU RITUALS

ISBN 0-688-16117-0 (paperback)

Offers more than seventy delightful rhymes and games that send the message of unconditional love and enhance children's social, emotional, and school success. Winner of a 1999 Parent's Guide Children's Media Award, these positive nursery rhymes, interactive finger plays, soothing games, and physically active can be played with children from infancy through age eight. *I Love You Rituals* gives parents, grandparents, caregivers, and teachers inspiring tools to help children thrive.

www.beckybailey.com